BLUEPRINTS
Early Years

Rhona Whiteford

Jim Fitzsimmons

Stanley Thornes (Publishers) Ltd

Do you receive BLUEPRINTS NEWS?

Blueprints is an expanding series of practical teacher's ideas books and photocopiable resources for use in primary schools. Books are available for separate infant and junior age ranges for every core and foundation subject, as well as for an ever widening range of other primary teaching needs. These include **Blueprints Primary English** books and **Blueprints Resource Banks**. **Blueprints** are carefully structured around the demands of the National Curriculum in England and Wales, but are used successfully by schools and teachers in Scotland, Northern Ireland and elsewhere.

Blueprints provide:
- *Total curriculum coverage*
- *Hundreds of practical ideas*
- *Books specifically for the age range you teach*
- *Flexible resources for the whole school or for individual teachers*
- *Excellent photocopiable sheets – ideal for assessment and children's work profiles*
- *Supreme value.*

Books may be bought by credit card over the telephone and information obtained on **(01242) 577944**. Alternatively, photocopy and return this **FREEPOST** form to receive **Blueprints News**, our regular update on all new and existing titles. You may also like to add the name of a friend who would be interested in being on the mailing list.

Please add my name to the **BLUEPRINTS NEWS** mailing list.

Mr/Mrs/Miss/Ms _____

Home address _____

_____ Postcode _____

School address _____

_____ Postcode _____

Please also send **BLUEPRINTS NEWS** to:

Mr/Mrs/Miss/Ms _____

Address _____

_____ Postcode _____

To: Marketing Services Dept., Stanley Thornes Ltd, FREEPOST (GR 782), Cheltenham, GL50 1BR

Text © Rhona Whiteford and Jim Fitzsimmons 1996

Original line illustrations by Debbie Clark © ST(P) Ltd 1996

First published in 1996
First published in new binding in 1998 by
Stanley Thornes (Publishers) Ltd
Ellenborough House
Wellington Street
CHELTENHAM GL50 1YW

99 00 / 10 9 8 7 6 5 4 3 2

A catalogue record for this book is available from the British Library.

ISBN 0–7487–3455–4

Typeset by Tech-Set, Gateshead, Tyne & Wear.
Printed and bound in Great Britain by
Redwood Books, Trowbridge, Wiltshire

INTRODUCTION

The *Early Years Book* is a photocopiable resource for all Early Years professionals with children aged between three and six. It provides basic material for all relevant areas of the curriculum working towards Level 1 of the National Curriculum. This includes pre-writing, reading and early number recording, as well as an introduction to science.

The book also includes special reminder pages. These are designed as short tests, or to consolidate work from previous pages. They could be used as an addition to a child's record of achievement, or as evidence to support written reports or comments.

This book also contains invaluable material for children's records, information to parents and a pre-school book.

The material can be used in a variety of ways, for example, enlarged for use with a group or for wall-display, incorporated into posters, friezes and letters, made into small booklets, or reduced to fit into existing books. The teacher's notes section outlines possible uses for the pages.

Written by experienced Early Years practitioners, the book is specifically designed for this age group both in content and appearance and will be an indispensible aid.

USING THE ACTIVITIES

MATHEMATICS

We have assumed that the children will have had much practical experience of making sets, sorting and classifying, using a variety of objects in the classroom. These sheets should be used as a means of recording this previous experience. They may be used for individuals, or enlarged to A3 size for group discussion or display.

Making a set
Copymaster 1
Use this sheet to show that members of a set go together. The child draws a ring around the things that are the same.

Make a set
Copymaster 2
Children make sets according to the property of colour or shape.

Draw a set
Copymasters 3, 4 and 5
Children use these sheets to draw a set of objects with two like properties. For example, on copymaster 3, balls which are yellow, and boats which are red; on copymaster 4, large and small apples; copymaster 5, tall and short flowers. These sheets also introduce suitable language for comparison.

Partitioning sets
Copymasters 6 and 7
These sheets are intended to encourage children to look at a whole set of similar objects and talk about ways in which they can partition them to make smaller groups or subsets.

Reminder page
Copymaster 8
On this reminder sheet, children are asked to draw sets of objects and divide a set of fruit into subsets.

Subsets
Copymaster 9
This set of vehicles can be partitioned in several ways, for example type, colour, shape or size, or in terms of movement on land, sea, air or space. Encourage the children to discuss how they would sort and classify each subset, and also to count the members of each subset.

Matching
Copymasters 10, 11 and 12
Use these sheets to record equivalence between sets as the child matches the members of one set with another and (on copymaster 12) makes his/her own sheet of matching things.

More than/less than
Copymaster 13
Once the child has had plenty of practical experience of the concept of more than and less than, this sheet can be used as a record of level of understanding.

Cardinal numbers 1–5
Copymasters 14–18
As before, we have assumed lots of previous practical experience of counting and handling quantities. These sheets are to give practice in recording the conservation of number, practice in number formation, and recognition and writing of the number word. If required, the sheets can be enlarged and displayed as part of a number frieze.

Draw the quantity
Copymaster 19
This sheet gives practice in drawing sets of a given number. An example of the set member is shown to help with drawing.

Numeral and word 1–5
Copymaster 20
This gives practice in writing the numerals and the word for numbers 1–5.

Reminder page
Copymaster 21
Use this as a follow-up to the work from previous pages to help consolidate the word, quantity and numeral work for the numbers 1–5. Children are asked to match up the numeral and the word to the correct quantity.

Ordering numbers
Copymaster 22
This sheet gives practice in the order and sequence of the numbers 1–5. It highlights the need to note the starting point in order to determine whether the sequence of numbers goes from left to right, or from right to left.

Dot-to-dot
Copymaster 23
This sheet gives more practice in ordering and the correct sequence of numbers. Children must follow a sequence of numbers (1–5) to complete the pictures.

Missing numbers
Copymaster 24
This sheet gives more practice in sequence and order of numbers 1–5. Children have to put in the missing numbers in a number line.

Cardinal numbers 6–10
Copymasters 25–29
As for the numbers 1–5, (Copymasters 14–18), the sheets give practice in recording number conservation, number formation, and recognition and writing of number words.

Draw the quantity
Copymaster 30
This sheet gives practice in drawing and colouring sets of objects of a given quantity.

Numeral and word 6–10
Copymaster 31
This gives practice in recognising and writing the numerals and the words for numbers 6–10.

Ordering and **Dot-to-dot**
Copymasters 32 and 33
These sheets help to consolidate the order and sequence of numbers from 1–10.

Reminder page
Copymaster 34
Children are asked to match up the numeral and the word to the correct quantity, for the numbers 6–10.

Add one more and **Take one away**
Copymasters 35 and 36
These sheets are intended as a record of introduction to basic addition and subtraction and should only be attempted after much practical experience in the classroom.

Mr Shape, 3D shape and **Spotting 3D shapes**
Copymasters 37, 38 and 39
Use these sheets as a record after the children have had plenty of practical experience handling 2D and 3D shapes. The sheets can be enlarged for use as part of a classroom display on 'Shape', or as the basis for class or group discussion.

Times of the day
Copymaster 40
These sheets can be used as part of a topic on 'Time'. Encourage discussion of other important times of the day, and use in conjunction with a large teaching clock with movable hands. Round up the times to the nearest hour, and discuss the position of the big hand and the little hand of the clock to show the time.

Comparing height and **Comparing capacity**
Copymasters 41 and 42
Work in small groups to discuss the position of things in relation to each other, and also give the children plenty of experience of pouring liquids from one container to another. When they have had lots of opportunities to discuss and observe, the sheets can be used to test their understanding of the concepts.

Reminder page
Copymaster 43
This gives further practice and consolidation of the previous pages relating to shape, size and capacity.

ENGLISH

Free lines
Copymaster 44
This sheet is intended to help develop good control and pencil grip in the youngest children or those experiencing particular difficulty. The teacher can write in the colours on the tubes for the child to follow or, in the case of older children, they can write in their own colours.

Directions/Left to right/Tracking/Mazes/Dot-to-dot patterns
Copymasters 45–49
All these sheets give practice in pencil control, direction, scanning across the page and matching, to help develop essential pre-writing skills. They could be photocopied and made into a small booklet for the children to take home and work on.

What can you see? and **Odd one out**
Copymasters 50 and 51
These sheets help to develop visual discrimination. On Copymaster 50, children are asked to colour the shapes in the large picture to match the shapes they can see below. Copymaster 51 asks children to spot the thing in each set which does not fit in with the others.

Alphabet
Copymasters 52–77
These individual sheets introduce the sounds of the letters of the alphabet. The illustrations introduce the idea of initial sounds supported by picture clues. There are two lines in which the children can practise letter formation before completing the last line of letters on their own.

The top half of the sheet could be coloured and

mounted onto card to make an alphabet frieze or for classroom display of chosen letters.

Sounds fountain and Sounds quilt
Copymasters 78 and 79
Use these sheets to give further practice in recognition and matching of the letters of the alphabet.

Reminder page
Copymaster 80
This sheet is a checklist of all the sounds of the letters of the alphabet. It can be used at several times during the term to record a child's progress in recognising those sounds.

Letter names 1 and 2
Copymasters 81 and 82
As above, these sheets can be used to record the child's ability to recognise and say the names of the letters of the alphabet (shown in lower case on copymaster 81 and capitals on copymaster 82). They can also be reduced and stuck into children's exercise books to help with the letter sequence of the alphabet, which is important when looking for words in simple dictionaries or wordbanks.

Initial sounds/Final sounds/Medial sounds
Copymasters 83–85
These sheets can be used as an aid to simple phonic analysis, and to help with word-building and word-attack skills. The picture clues are to help the children put the missing letters in the boxes.

Words and pictures/matching words
Copymasters 86 and 87
Use these sheets to help develop recognition of common words. On copymaster 86 children should join the words to the pictures and copy out the words. On copymaster 87 they should draw lines to join matching words. Both sheets can be enlarged and used in vocabulary displays in the classroom. Copymaster 86 could be enlarged, stuck onto card and made into an interactive display by cutting out small cards to fit over the blank spaces. If the words from the sheet are written on the smaller cards the children can physically match the words. In this way the sheet can be used many times.

Opposites
Copymaster 88
The children are asked to match the words which are opposites by drawing a line. The pictures are visual clues to help them.

Rhyming words
Copymaster 89
The work on this sheet is designed to help listening skills and develop aural discrimination, again using word recognition and visual clues to join the words which rhyme with each other with a line.

Tell a story
Copymaster 90
This sheet is designed to encourage observation and discussion, and also to promote understanding of the need for a sequence of events in storytelling. For small-group work the sheet can be enlarged and cut up. Children can be encouraged to tell the story with the teacher acting as scribe. The pictures and numbers can be fixed to a white board with Blu-tak®. More able children can cut out the pictures and stick them in sequence on a sheet of paper themselves, older children could try to write the story as well.

Picture clues
Copymaster 91
Use this sheet to help develop word recognition and response to visual clues in text as an aid to reading. A space is left next to each picture for the children to select and copy the correct word from the wordbank.

SCIENCE

I look like this
Copymaster 92
Children can use this sheet to record personal visual characteristics. When completed it can be used as part of a study of similarities and differences within a class or group.

Things I can do
Copymaster 93
This sheet can be used as a record of a child's skills and abilities. It can be kept as a record over a period of time as the child ticks off the skills as they acquire them.

The body
Copymaster 94
Introduce the names of the different parts of the body over a period of time. The sheet can be enlarged, filled in by the teacher and used as part of the classroom display. Individual sheets can then be issued to the children to test their knowledge.

Living and non-living things
Copymaster 95
Make a collection of a variety of things, both living and non-living, to give the children lots of opportunity to talk about the concept. Collect pictures and ask the children to sort and classify them. Finally, use the sheet for the children to make a set of living things by drawing a circle around them. You could add to the collection with objects made from things that were once alive; for example, wood and leather. Older children could try to sort out those things from the rest of the objects.

Similarities and differences
Copymaster 96
Use this sheet as a comparison between two individuals to promote observation and discussion. The sheets can be used as part of a study of similarities and differences within a class or group.

Colours
Copymaster 97
Children are asked to match the colours and numbers, and then scan the page to help them colour in the picture.

What plants need to live and **Growing things**
Copymasters 98 and 99
These sheets can be used to record the best conditions for good plant growth. Copymaster 98 asks the children to draw in the three most important things most plants need to live – water, soil and sunshine. Make sure the children have opportunities to observe what happens to a plant if any or all of these are not provided. Copymaster 99 can be used to record a simple growing experiment. You can pose the question 'Do plants always need soil to grow?'

All kinds of food
Copymaster 100
This sheet can be used to highlight foods for different purposes. The children can draw on the plate, for example, those foods which give us energy, or foods which build us up. The drawings around the edge of the sheet will provide some ideas. Alternatively, enlarge the sheets and ask the children to draw in favourite foods for breakfast, lunch and dinner, or create a favourite meal. This can be used as part of a class display.

Keeping clean and healthy
Copymaster 101
These sheets can be completed by the children and then used as a basis for a discussion about healthy lifestyles or for gathering information for a graph.

Weather and clothes and **Seasons and change**
Copymasters 102-104
Use these sheets to highlight changes brought about by the seasons of the year. Discuss the changes which affect the children especially. On copymasters 103 and 104, the children can draw themselves involved in a seasonal activity, or draw the wildlife that might be seen at that time of the year, or in that habitat.

Heating changes and **Cooling changes**
Copymasters 105 and 106
Give the children lots of opportunities to observe changes brought about by heating and cooling so that they can complete the sheets from direct observation as much as possible. They should draw lines from the materials at the top of the page, through the agent of change, to match up with the changed state of the material at the bottom.

Look for litter and pollution
Copymaster 107
Use this sheet to promote observation and discussion about litter and pollution in the environment. Take the children out for a walk around school or in your local area and encourage them to look for evidence of these things. Try to take some photographs of the worst examples for inclusion in a class display. Older children could try to design anti-litter or anti-pollution posters for display around the school.

Light and shadow
Copymaster 108
Go outside on a sunny day and have fun making shadows; alternatively use torches in a dark area of the classroom. Encourage the children to observe the way shadows are made, and to notice that most of the time the shadows look very much like the object to which they belong. Children can then complete the sheet by ticking and colouring the things which have the correct shadow. Older children can experiment further by trying to make shadows which look nothing like the object at all.

Collecting materials
Copymaster 109
Make a collection of a variety of materials and cut these into small pieces. Encourage observation and discussion of the properties of the different materials. Children can then choose samples to stick onto the appropriate box on the sheet.

Loud and soft sounds and **How sounds are made**
Copymasters 110 and 111
If possible, try to gather together all the things illustrated on the sheets, or alternatively make tape-recordings. Give the children a chance to listen to the sounds and encourage discussion. Most of the instruments illustrated on copymaster 111 should be easily available, and the children should be given a chance to make sounds on the instruments themselves. Talk about the way in which the sounds are usually made, but encourage discussion and experimentation of different ways of making them.

Air power
Copymaster 112
This is a simple sorting and classifying exercise, but the children will enjoy going outside to test some things which are moved by air.

Water power
Copymaster 113
Collect the things illustrated on the sheet and let the children try the activity for themselves (preferably outside). Children complete the sheet by ticking those things they were able to move using water squeezed from a washing-up-liquid bottle.

Floating and sinking
Copymaster 114
Collect together all the things illustrated on the sheet and let the children test which things float and which

things sink in the tank of water. Encourage the children to place the objects on the surface of the water carefully, then not so carefully so see if this makes any difference. Try to encourage the children to give reasons why the objects either float or sink, and why some objects do not sink straight to the bottom.

Magnet power
Copymaster 115

Set up a small table with several magnets and a collection of small items made from different materials. Try to include the ones illustrated on the sheet, so the children can experiment for themselves. They can then complete the sheet by joining with a line all those things that were attracted to the magnet.

Pushes and pulls
Copymaster 116

Collect together the items as illustrated and let the children play with them. Talk about the difference between a push and a pull and encourage the children to think about how they make the things move. Talk about the parts of the body they use and how some of the objects may need both a push and a pull. Use the sheet to record their observations.

Safety in the home – Electricity
Copymaster 117

The children could take this sheet home and work on it with parents. They could also identify any potentially hazardous things in their own homes.

STARTING SCHOOL

The following sheets can be used as part of a pre-school booklet, or as an initial diagnostic booklet to test some of the basic skills upon entry to school or nursery, or upon leaving nursery or playgroup.

I know these colours
Copymaster 118

I can write my name
Copymaster 119

I know these numbers
Copymaster 120

I can draw a special picture
Copymaster 121

Things I can do
Copymaster 123

I can draw myself
Copymaster 123

Welcome to school
Copymaster 124

Things needed for school
Copymaster 125

Medical/home information sheet
Copymaster 126

Diary
Copymasters 127 and 128

Many schools and nurseries have found it extremely useful to keep an anecdotal diary on some children. In many cases this has helped to foster closer home/school links and has been found to be particularly useful in helping to create a holistic view of the child. The School diary (copymaster 127) can be used to record times of particular difficulty, or learning milestones and moments of special achievement. The Home diary (copymaster 128) can be completed by the parents or guardians to record responses to special events or celebrations, or skills learnt at home.

Information for parents
Copymaster 129

This sheet will provide parents with important information such as staff names, organisation of the school day, and procedures for collecting children. It is also useful for temporary visitors to school, such as supply teachers or medical personnel. The space at the top is for the school name and/or logo. Details can be added by hand or typed in the spaces provided. Parts of the sheet which are not required can be blanked out during photocopying.

My reading record
Copymaster 130

Blank out the left-hand part of the sheet when photocopying to make the cover of the reading record folder. This can be enlarged if desired. Blank out the right-hand part of the sheet and photocopy the reading record charts. Make as many copies of this as you will need. Staple the sheets into the cover to make a booklet. The reading record can be as large or small as you wish, and last for just a week or for a term. For greater durability the cover sheet could be stuck onto card.

Basic mathematics skills and Basic English skills
Copymasters 131 and 132

These basic checklists can be circled or ticked to show that a child has had experience of the various concepts. Kept by the teacher, they can be used as an aid for differentiation and assessment.

Make a set

Draw a ring around the things which are the same.

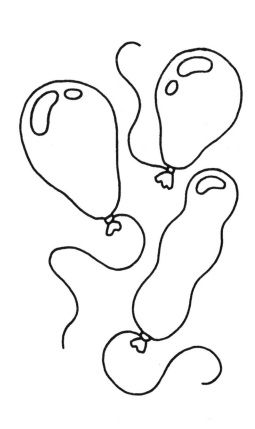

Make a set

Colour these fruits and then draw a ring around the fruits which are red.

Colour the squares blue, the circles yellow and the triangles green.

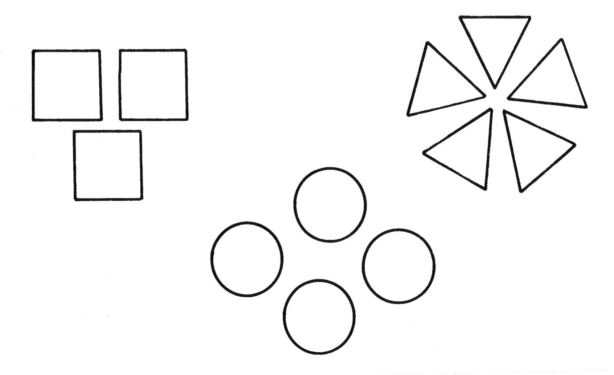

Make a set of blue squares.

Draw a set

Draw a set of yellow balls in the basket.

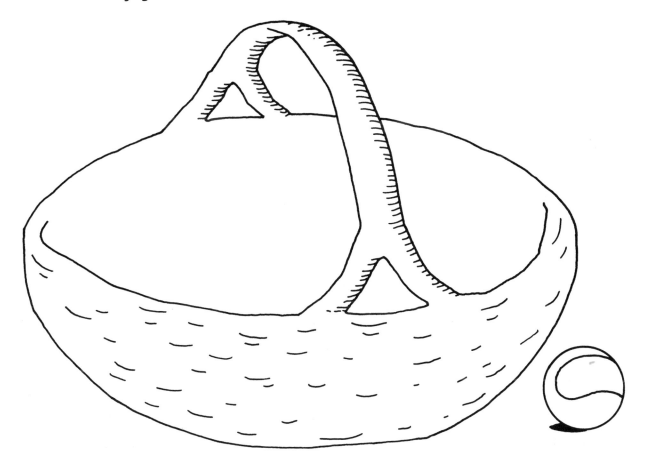

Draw a set of red boats on the pond.

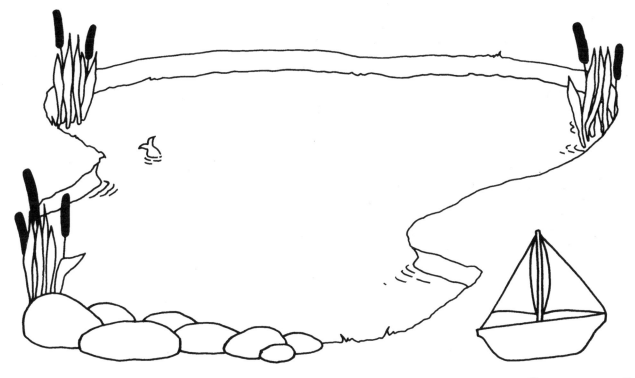

Draw a set

Draw a set of large apples on one tree and a set of small apples on the other tree.

Draw a set

Draw a set of tall flowers in the vase on the left. Draw a set of short flowers in the vase on the right.

Toy shop

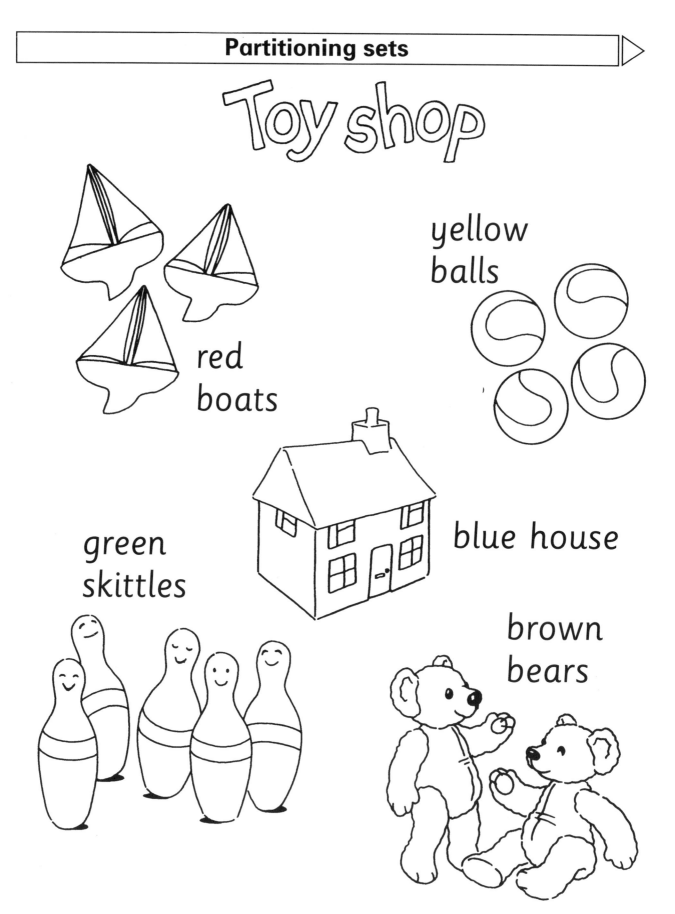

red boats

yellow balls

green skittles

blue house

brown bears

Draw a ring around this set of toys.
Draw a line between each subset.

All of these animals live on a farm. Sort them into sets and colour each set a different colour.

Reminder page

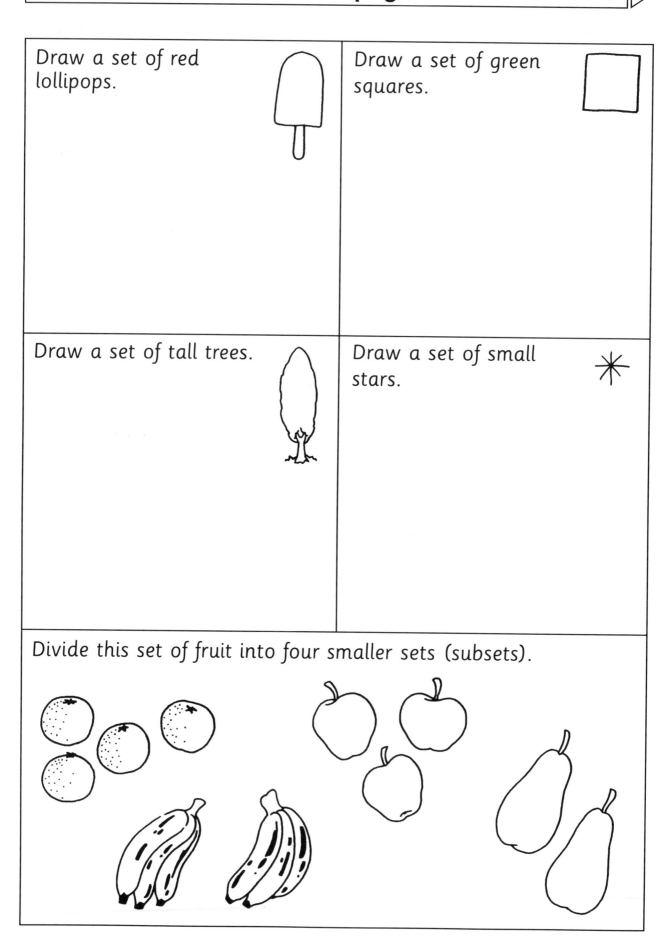

Draw a set of red lollipops.

Draw a set of green squares.

Draw a set of tall trees.

Draw a set of small stars.

Divide this set of fruit into four smaller sets (subsets).

Subsets

Make subsets from this set of vehicles.

How many in each subset?

Give each child a sweet.

Give each dog a bone.

Give each bird a worm.

Is there a cake for each child?

yes | no

Is there a hat for each clown?

yes | no

Is there a collar for each dog?

yes | no

Matching

Give each child a balloon.

Draw a sausage on each plate.

Put a cherry on each cake.

More than/less than

Colour the bowl which has more fruit red.
Colour the bowl which has less fruit blue.

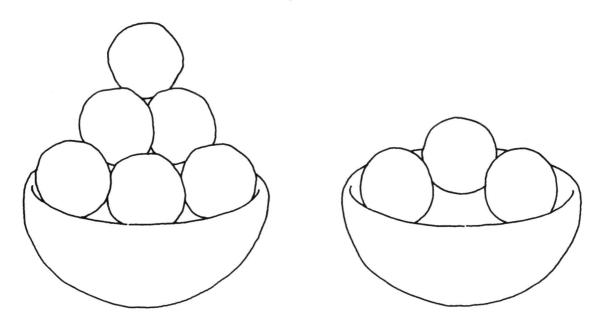

Colour the vase with more flowers yellow. Colour the vase with less flowers green.

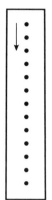

one

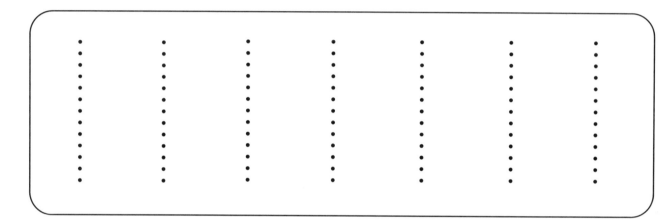

Colour the set of 1.

two

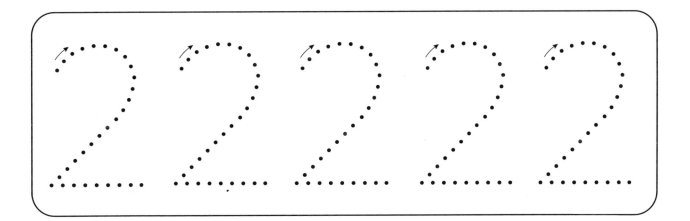

Colour the set of 2.

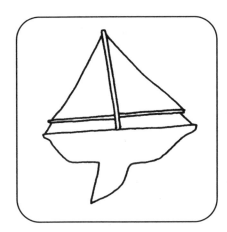 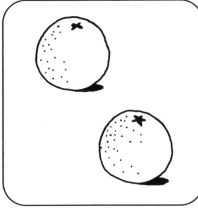 

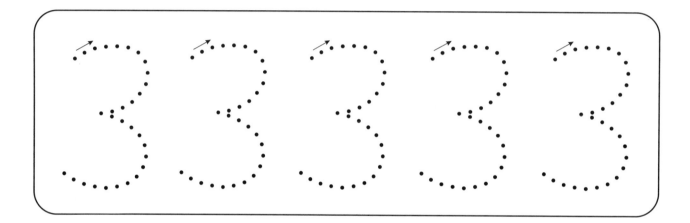

Colour the set of 3.

four

Colour the set of 4.

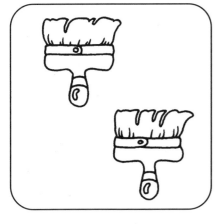

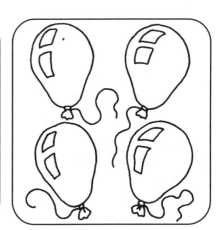

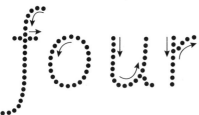

five

Colour the set of 5.

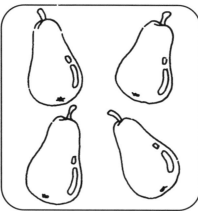

Draw the quantity

Draw the number of things in each set and then colour them in.

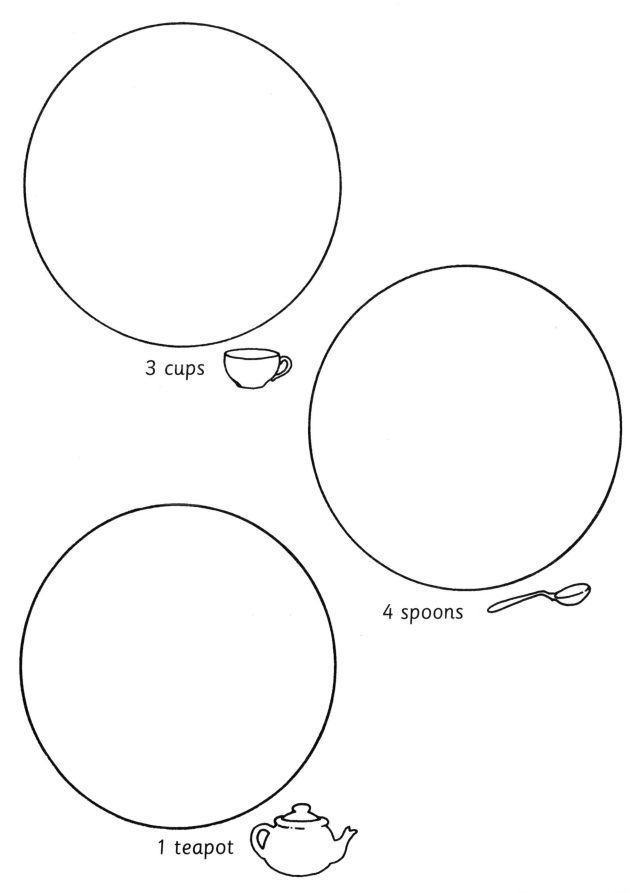

3 cups

4 spoons

1 teapot

Numeral and word 1–5

Write the numeral and the word under each set.

1	2	3	4	5
one	two	three	four	five

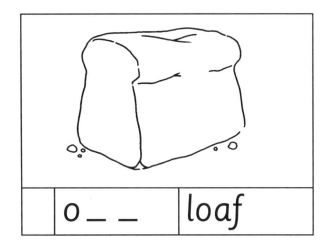

| o _ _ | loaf |

| t _ _ | ices |

| t _ _ _ _ | jellies |

| f _ _ _ | cakes |

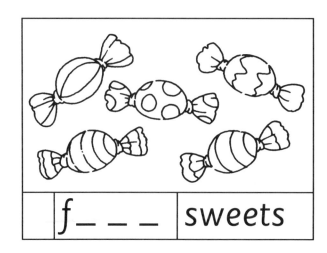

| f _ _ _ | sweets |

Draw lines to match the dominoes with the correct number and the correct number word.

4

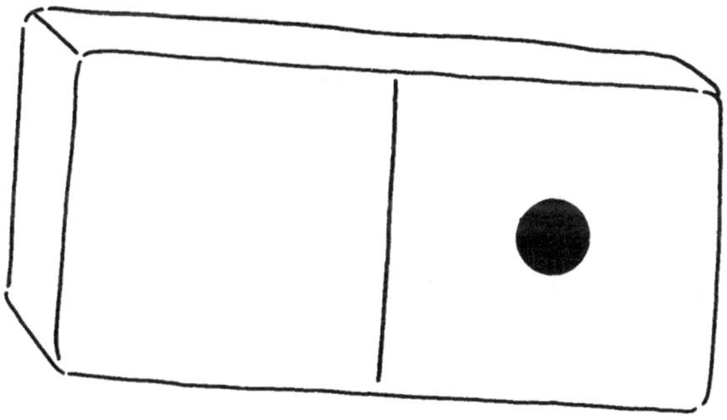

three

3

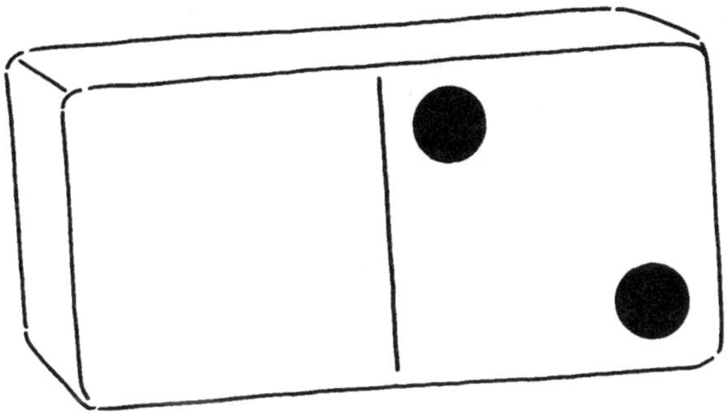

one

2

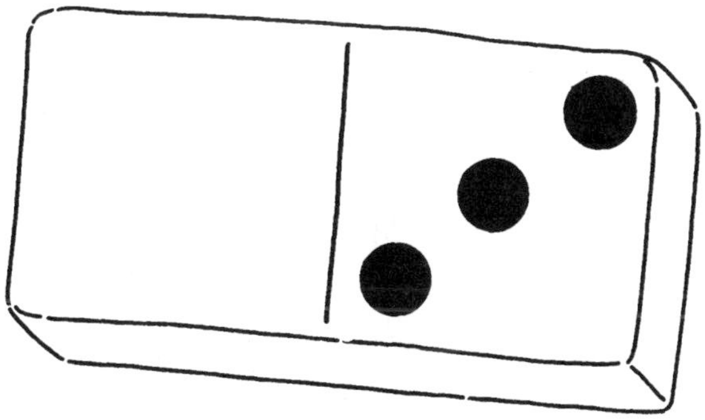

five

5

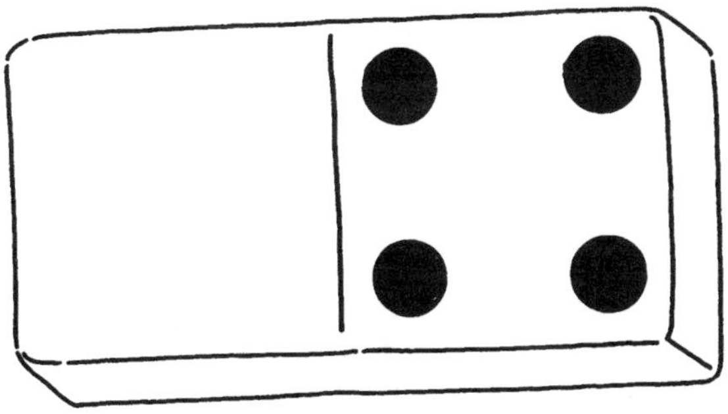

two

1

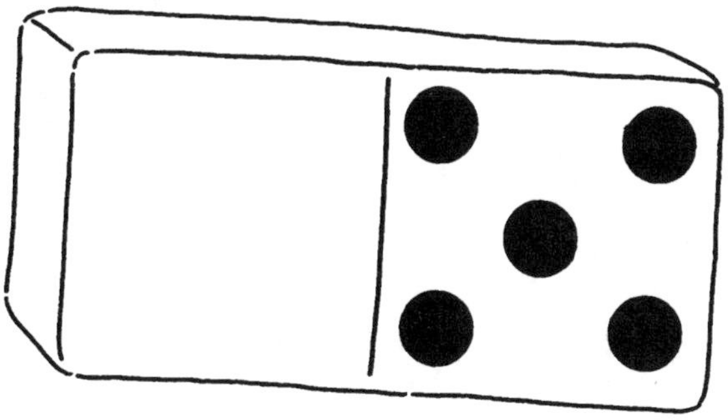

four

Number these carriages from the engine.

Number these cars from the traffic lights.

Number these boats from the lighthouse.

Dot-to-dot 1–5

Join the dots to complete the pictures.

Put in the missing numbers.

1	2	3	4	5

1   2

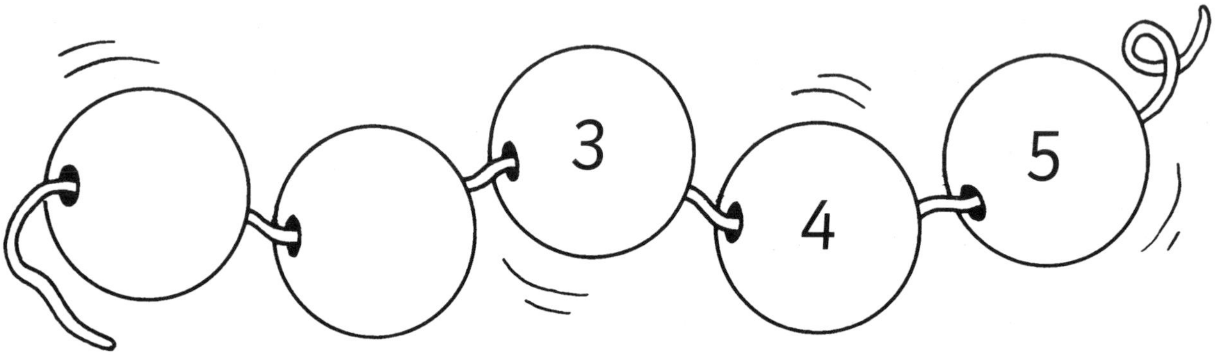

3   4   5

1   5

2   4

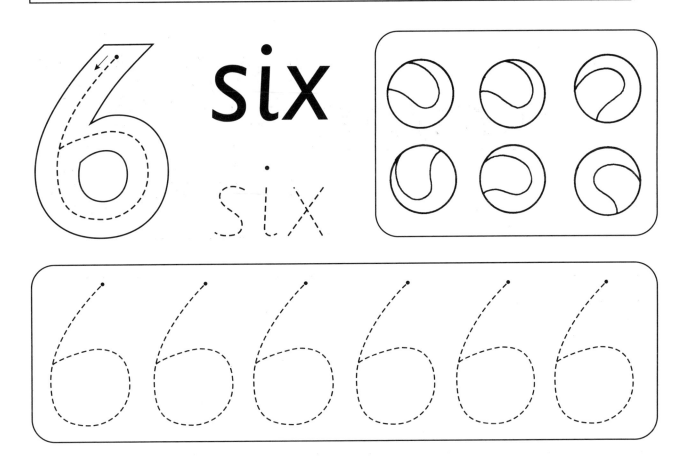

six

six

Colour the set of six.

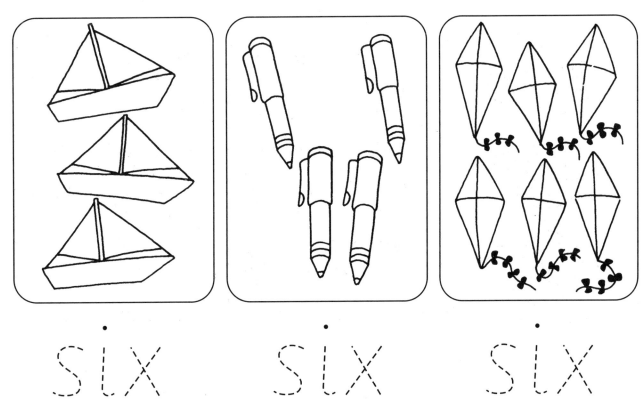

six   six   six

7 seven

Colour the set of seven.

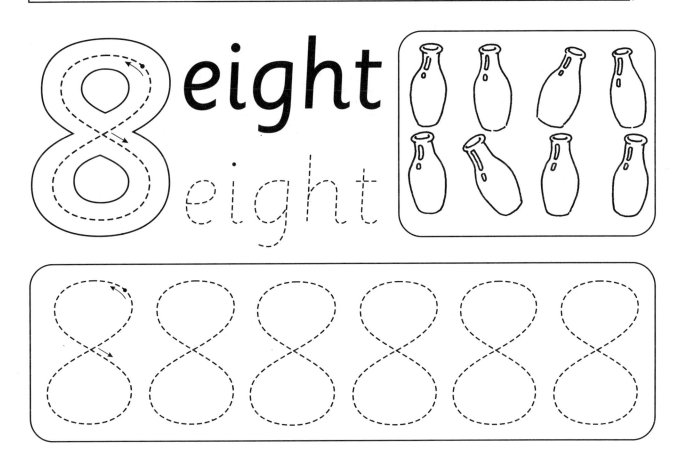

eight

eight

8 8 8 8 8 8

Colour the set of eight.

eight eight eight

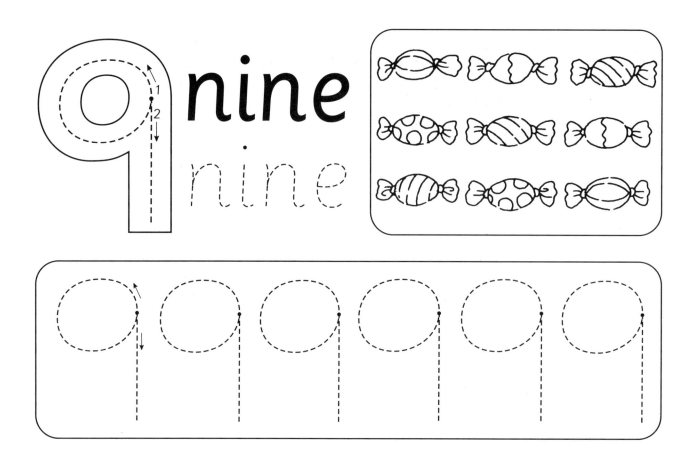

9 nine

nine

Colour the set of nine.

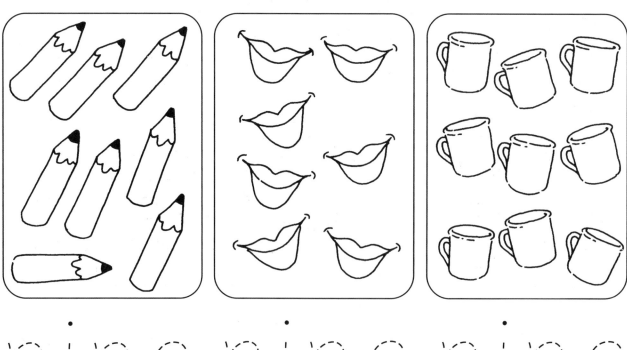

nine nine nine

10 ten

Colour the set of ten.

ten   ten   ten

Draw the quantity

Draw and colour the number of things in each set.

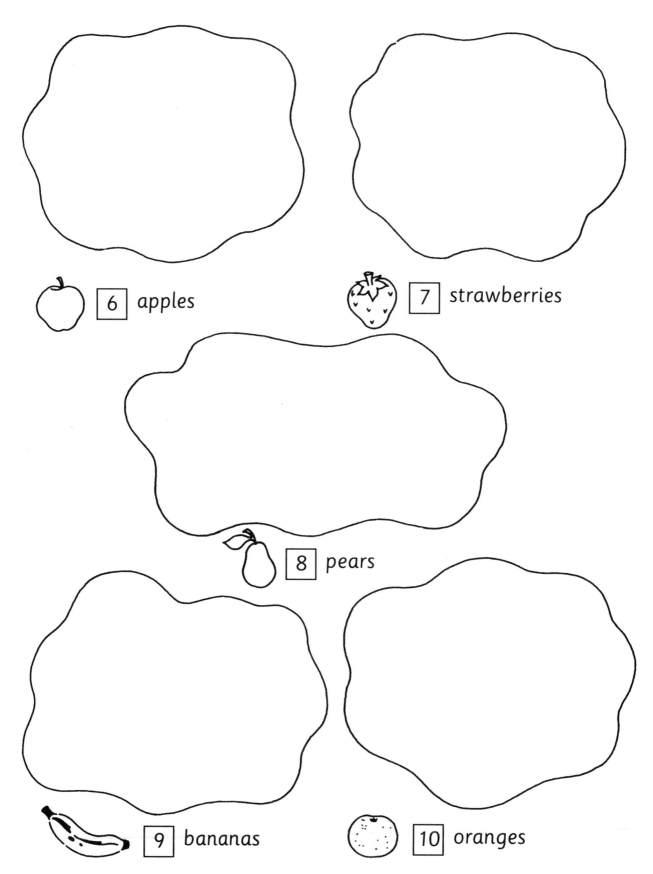

6 apples

7 strawberries

8 pears

9 bananas

10 oranges

Numerals and words 6–10

Write the numeral and the word under each set.

6	7	8	9	10
six	seven	eight	nine	ten

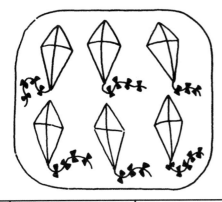

	s _ _	kites

	s _ _ _ _	bats

	e _ _ _ _	skittles

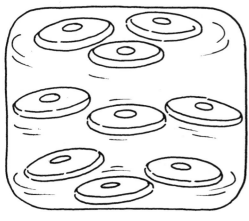

	n _ _ _	frisbees

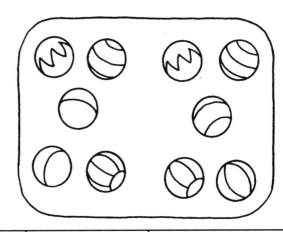

	t _ _	balls

| 1 | 2 | 3 | 4 | 5 | 6 | 7 | 8 | 9 | 10 |

Number these beads. Start from the arrow.

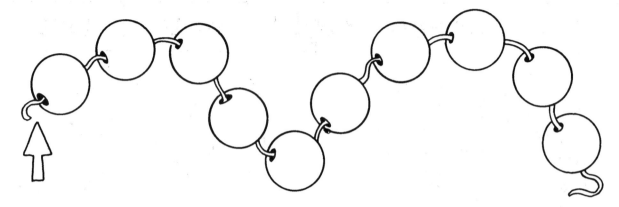

Number these cards. Start from the dot.

Put the missing numbers on these two rows of counters.

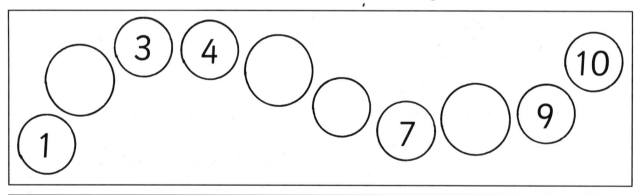

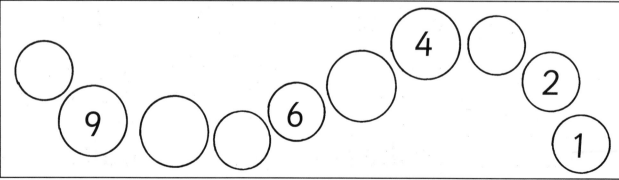

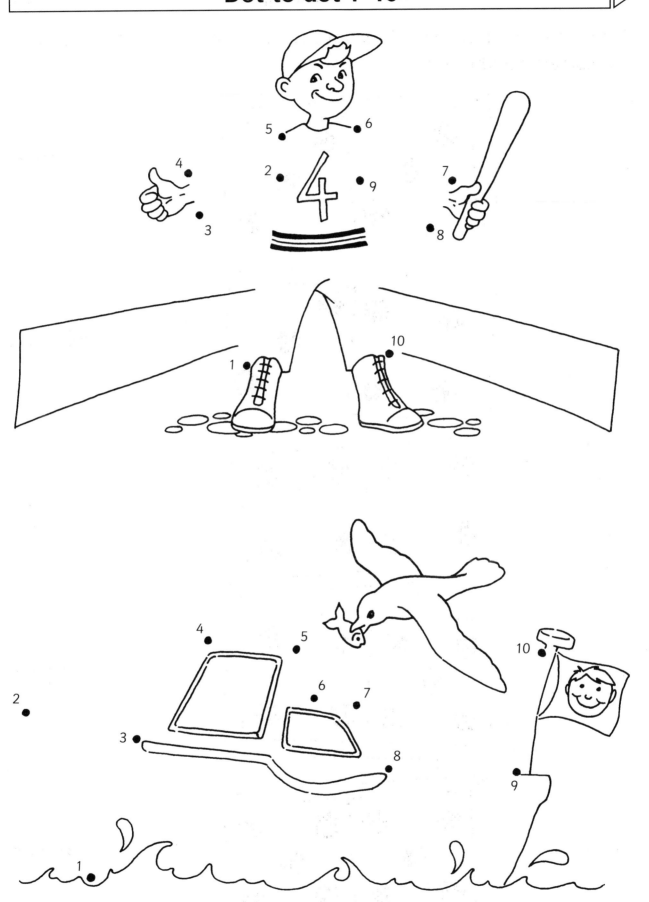

Draw lines to match the dominoes with the correct number and
the correct number word.

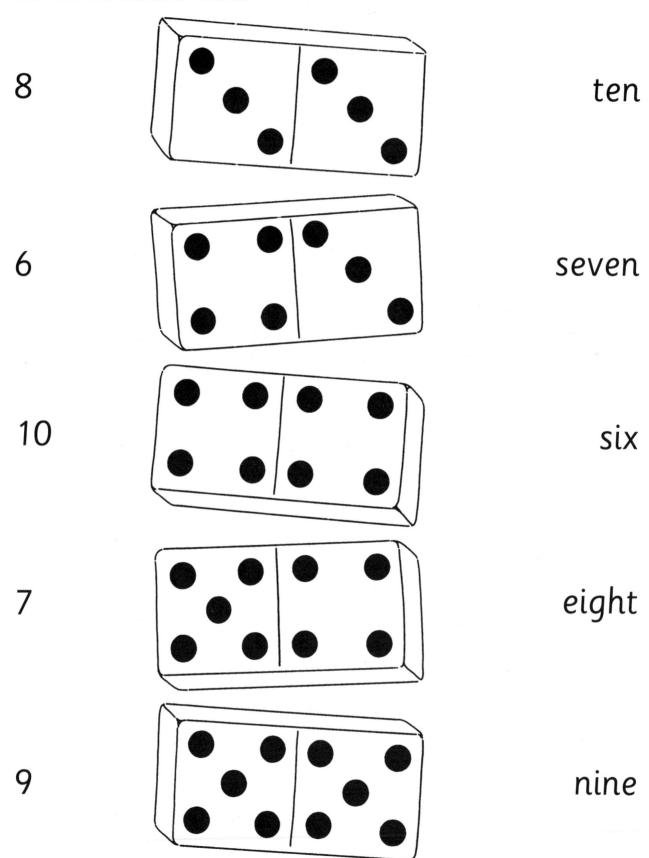

8
6
10
7
9

ten
seven
six
eight
nine

Add one more

Here are 3 ice creams.   Draw 1 more.   How many are there now?

Here are 4 sweets.   Draw 1 more.   How many are there now?

Here are 5 buns.   Draw 1 more.   How many are there now?

Here are 6 chocolate buttons.   Draw 1 more.   How many are there now?

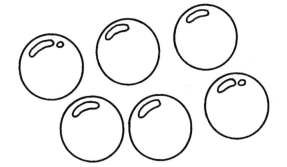

Here are 6 balls.   Take 1 away.   How many are there now?

Here are 5 hats.   Take 1 away.   How many are there now?

Here are 4 coats.   Take 1 away.   How many are there now?

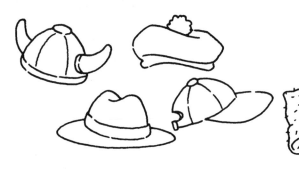

Here are 3 pairs of trousers.   Take 1 away.   How many are there now?

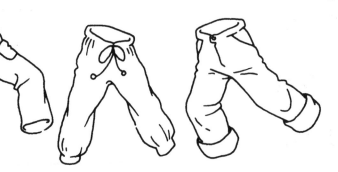

Colour the triangles △ red

Colour the circles ◯ blue

Colour the squares ☐ green

Colour the rectangles ▭ yellow

Colour the hexagons ⬡ orange

cylinder	pyramid	cube
cone	cuboid	sphere

Write the correct word next to these shapes.

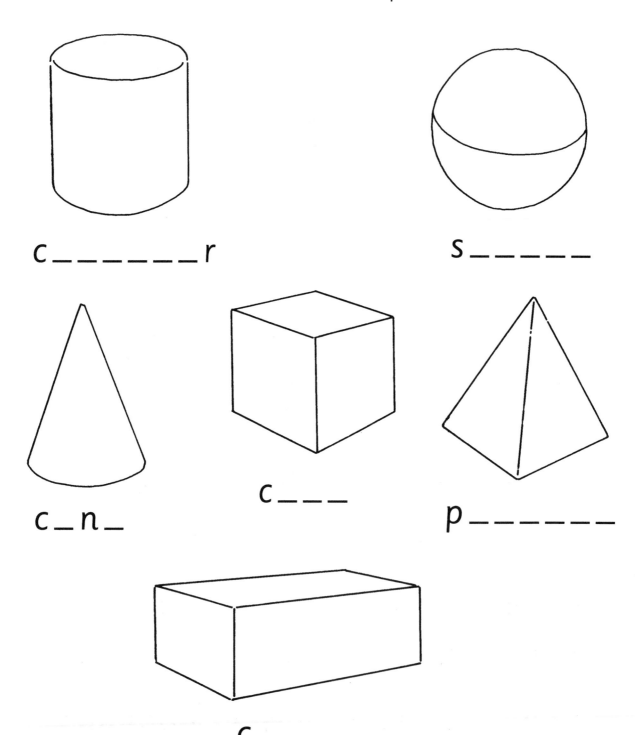

c _ _ _ _ _ _ r

s _ _ _ _ _

c _ n _

c _ _ _

p _ _ _ _ _ _

c _ _ _ _ _

Spotting 3D shapes

Tick the box if you can see the shape ✓

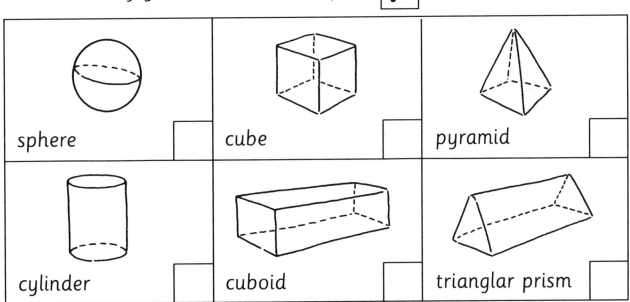

sphere ☐ cube ☐ pyramid ☐

cylinder ☐ cuboid ☐ trianglar prism ☐

Times of the day

I get up at _____ o-clock

I have my lunch at _____ o-clock

I go to bed at _____ o-clock

Copymaster 40

Comparing height

Complete the labels using these words.

| **highest** | **lowest** | **tallest** | **shortest** |

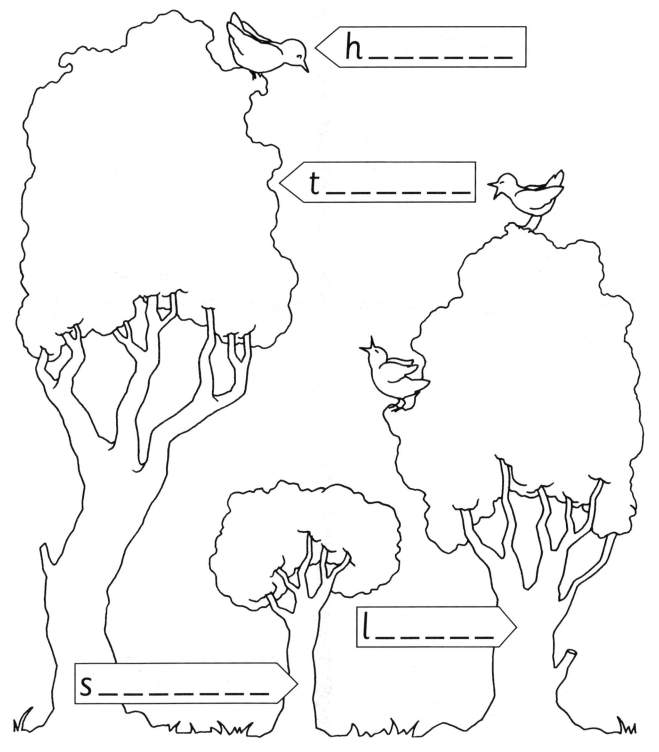

h _ _ _ _ _ _

t _ _ _ _ _ _

l _ _ _ _ _

s _ _ _ _ _ _ _

Comparing capacity

Tick the one which holds more

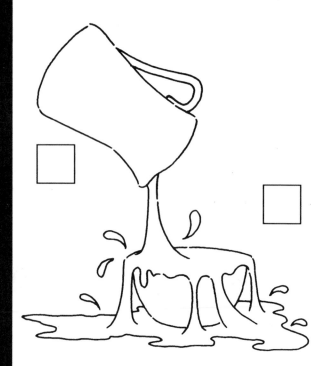

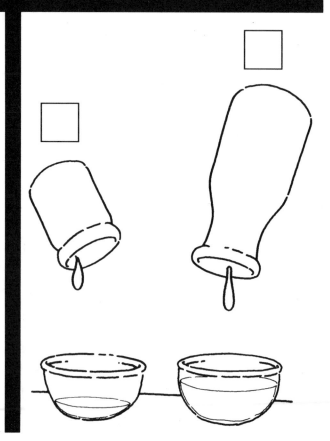

Colour the circle blue. Colour the triangle red.

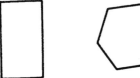 

Colour the cuboid green. Colour the sphere yellow.

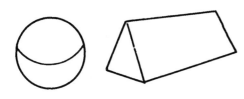

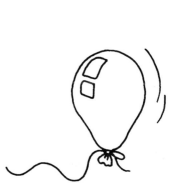

Colour the tallest tree green.

Colour the shortest tree blue.

Colour the highest balloon orange.

Colour the lowest balloon brown.

Tick the one which holds more.

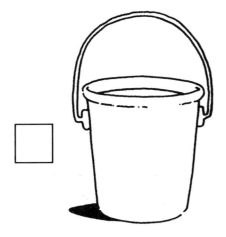

Free lines

Pick four colours and write them on the four tubes.
Take lines of the colours for a walk all over the page.

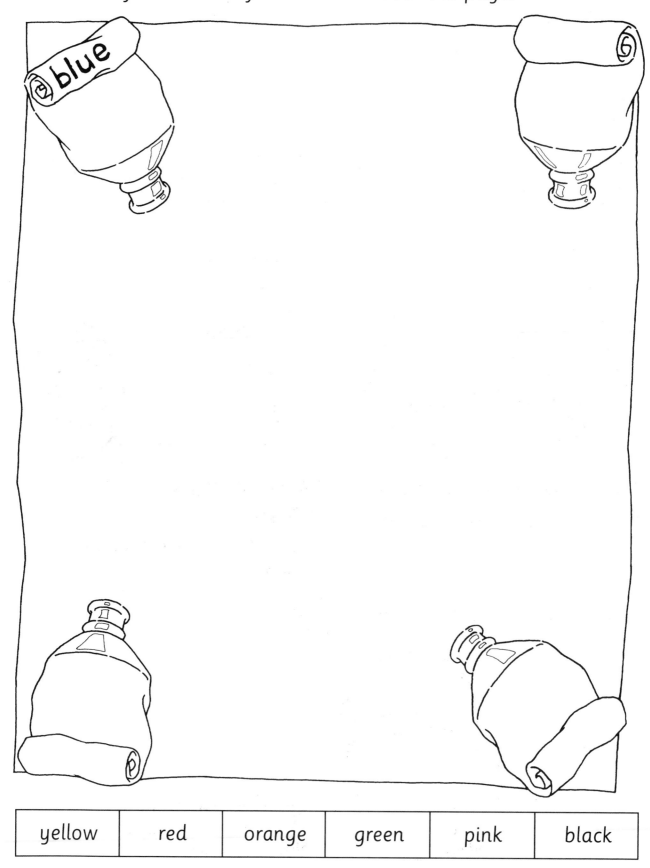

| yellow | red | orange | green | pink | black |

Put the stripes on these flying carpets.

Left to right

Land each spaceship on a planet.

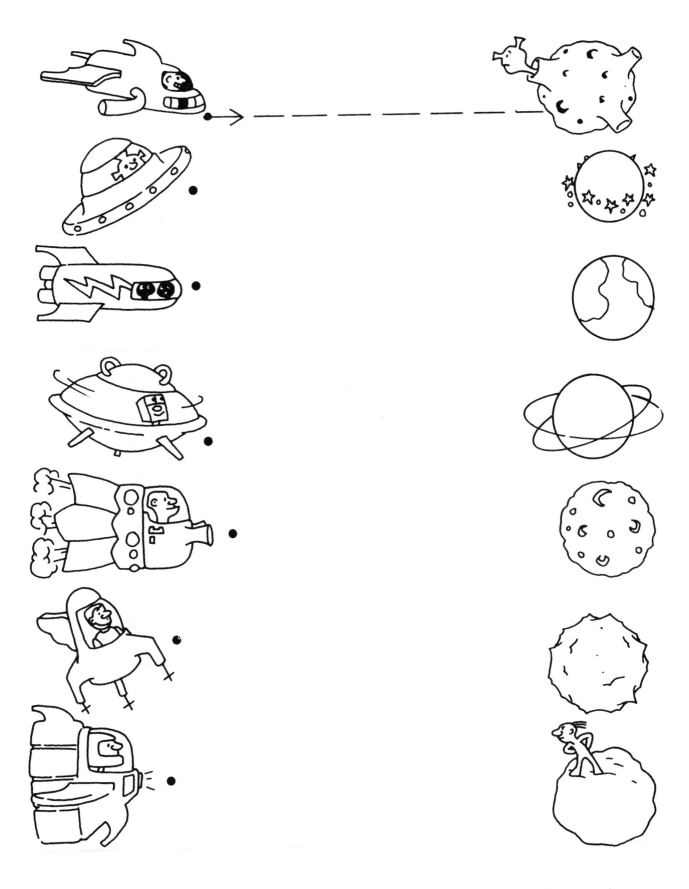

Tracking

Draw a line to take the mountaineer to the top of the mountain and then down the ski-slope.

Take the wolf to the little pig's house.

Take Robin Hood to his hide-out.

Dot-to-dot patterns

Complete the pattern on the tent using a different colour for each line.

In the boxes below, tick the shapes which you can see in the big picture above.

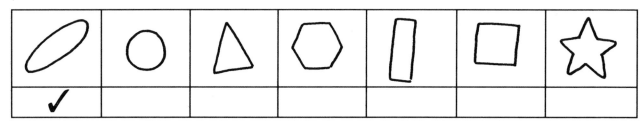

In the boxes below, tick the shapes which you can see in the big picture above.

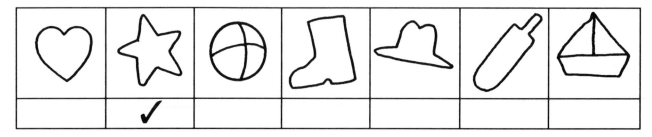

Odd one out

Colour the odd one out in each row.

  apple

Colour the pictures which start with the sound **a**.

  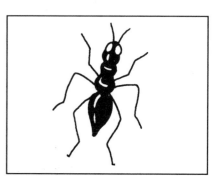

 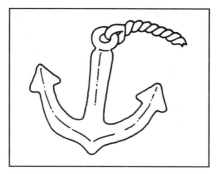 

a a a a a a a

a a a a a a a

a

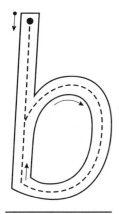

ball

Colour the pictures which start with the sound **b**.

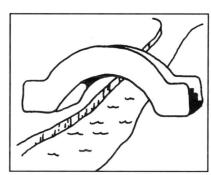

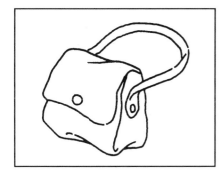
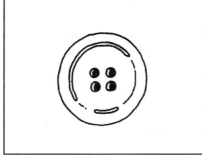
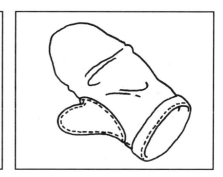

b b b b b b b

b b b b b b b

b

clown

Colour the pictures which start with the sound **C**.

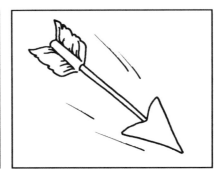

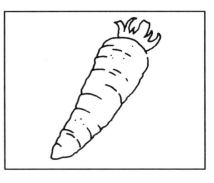

C C C C C C C

C C C C C C C

C

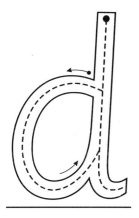

duck

Colour the pictures which start with the sound **d**.

 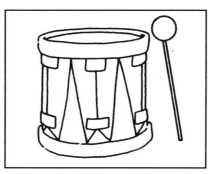 

d d d d d d

d d d d d d

d

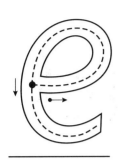

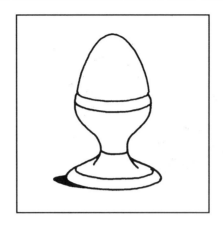

egg

Colour the pictures which start with the sound **e**.

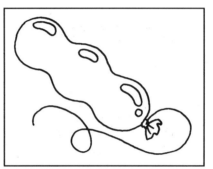

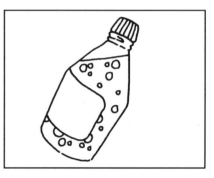

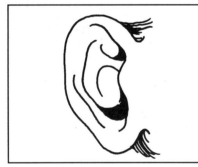

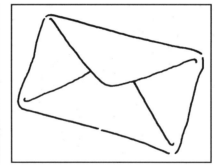

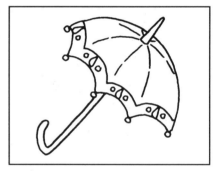

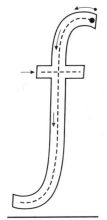 

fork

Colour the pictures which start with the sound **f**.

  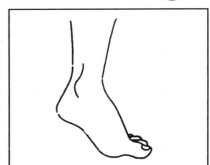

  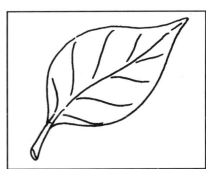

f f f f f f f f f

f f f f f f f f f

f

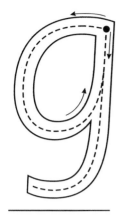

ghost

Colour the pictures which start with the sound **g**.

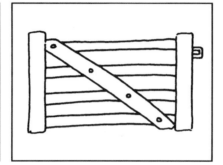

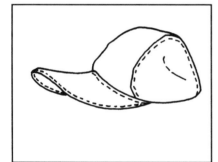

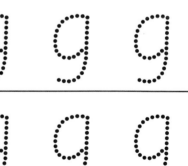

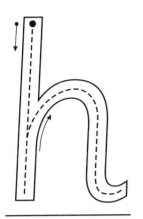

hat

Colour the pictures which start with the sound **h**.

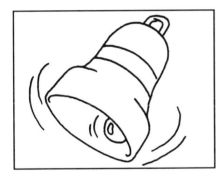

h h h h h h h

h h h h h h h

h

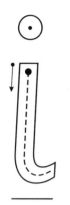

ink

Colour the pictures which start with the sound **i**.

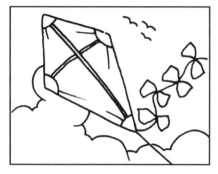

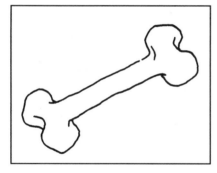

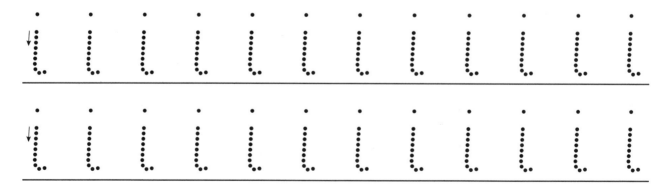

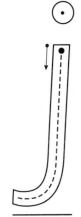

jam

Colour the pictures which start with the sound **j**.

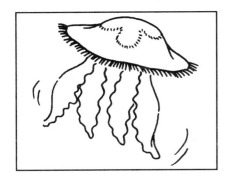

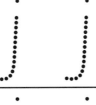

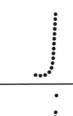

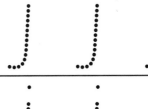

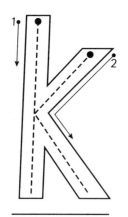

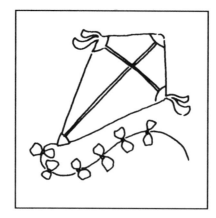

kite

Colour the pictures which start with the sound **k**.

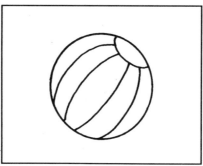

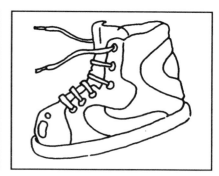

k k k k k k k

k k k k k k k

k

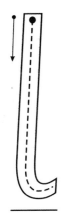

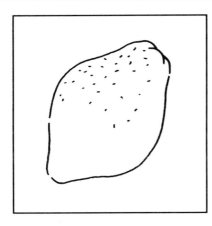

lemon

Colour the pictures which start with the sound **l**.

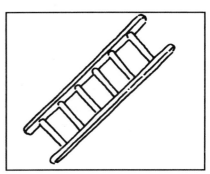

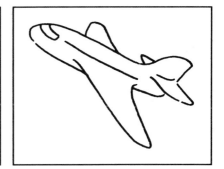

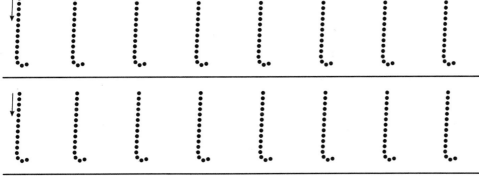

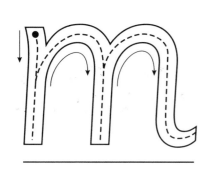  **man**

Colour the pictures which start with the sound **m**.

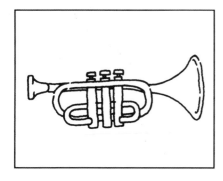  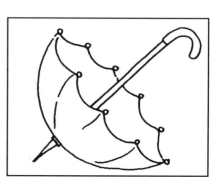

m m m m m m m m m m

m m m m m m m m m m

m

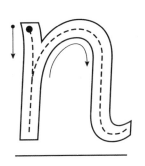
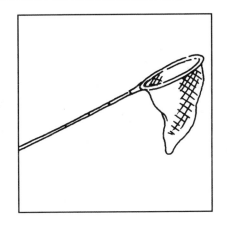

net

Colour the pictures which start with the sound **n**.

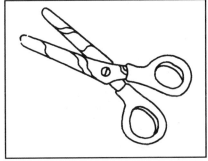

n n n n n n n n n

n n n n n n n n n

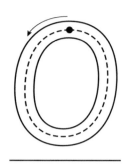 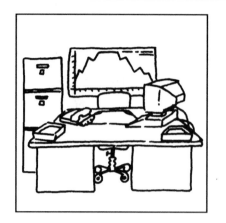

office

Colour the pictures which start with the sound **o**.

 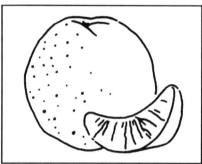 

 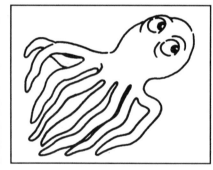 

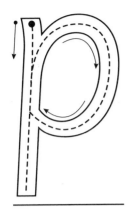 

pie

Colour the pictures which start with the sound **p**.

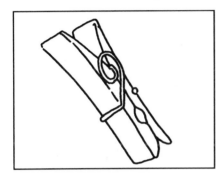 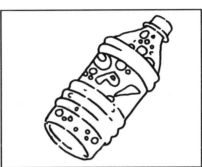 

queue

Colour the pictures which start with the sound q.

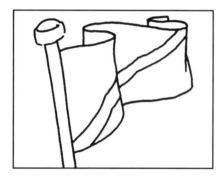

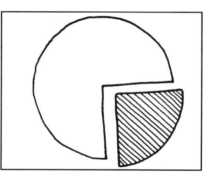

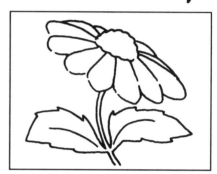

r

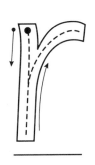 ring

Colour the pictures which start with the sound **r**.

 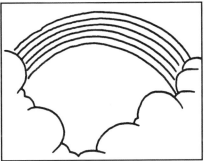 

r r r r r r r

r r r r r r r

sun

Colour the pictures which start with the sound **S**.

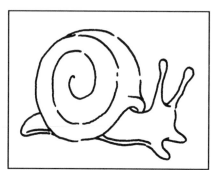

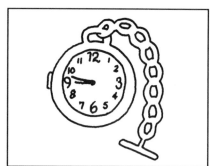

S S S S S S S

S S S S S S S

S

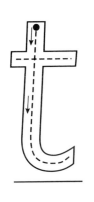  tomato

Colour the pictures which start with the sound **t**.

  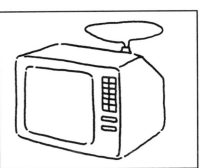

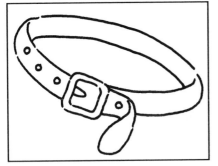  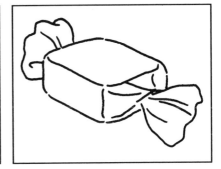

t t t t t t t t

t t t t t t t t

t

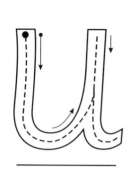 

unhappy

Colour the pictures which start with the sound **u**.

  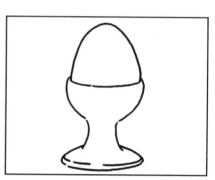

 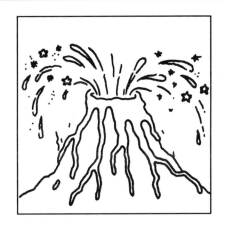 volcano

Colour the pictures which start with the sound **V**.

 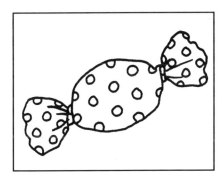 

  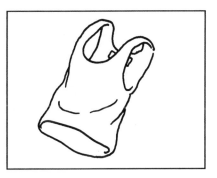

V V V V V V V V

V V V V V V V V

witch

Colour the pictures which start with the sound **w**.

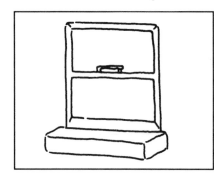  

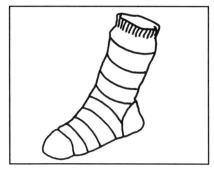  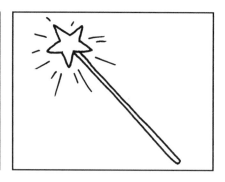

w w w w w w

w w w w w w

w

 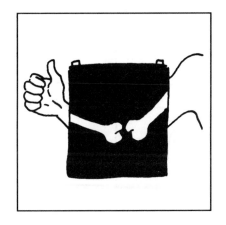 x-ray

Colour the pictures which end with the sound **X**.

 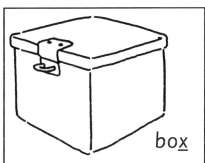 box

 fox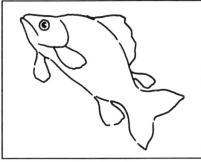

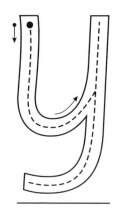 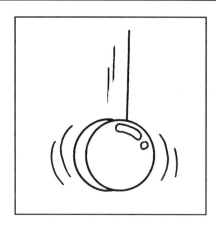

yo-yo

Colour the pictures which start with the sound **y**.

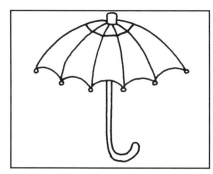  

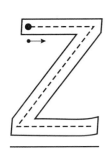  **zoom**

Colour the pictures which start with the sound **Z**.

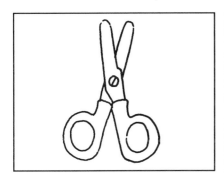 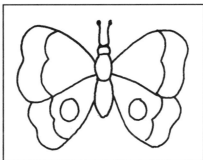 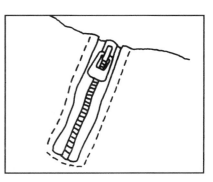

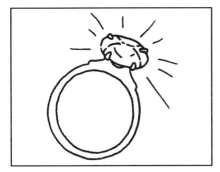  

Z Z Z Z Z Z Z

Z Z Z Z Z Z Z

Z

Sounds fountain

Join the matching sounds. Start at the arrow.

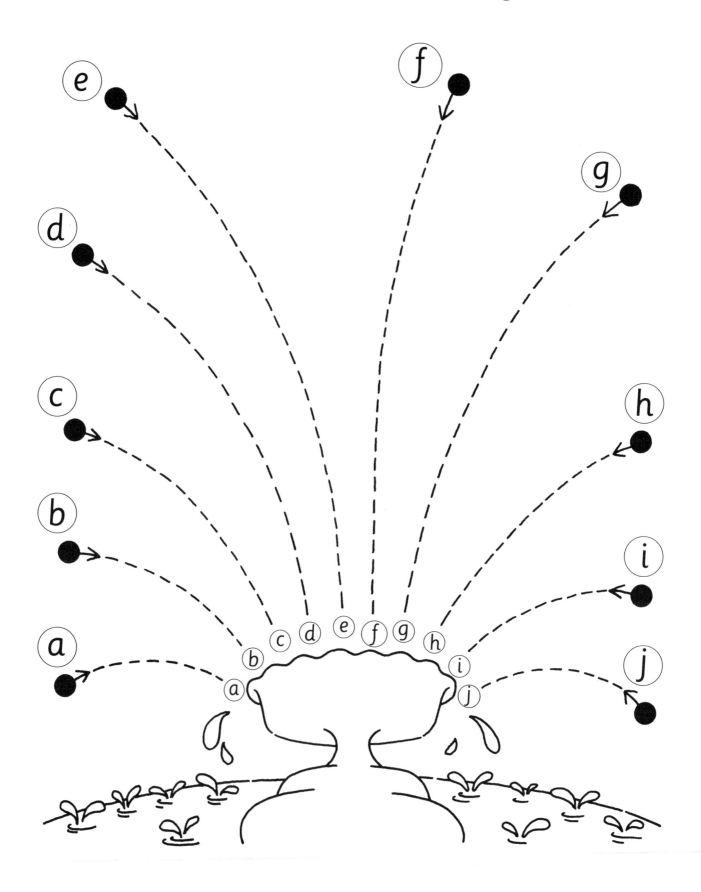

Sounds quilt

Join the matching sounds. Start at the arrow.

Colour in the sounds that you know.

a	b	c	d
e	f	g	h
i	j	k	l
m	n	o	p
q	r	s	t
u	v	w	fo**x** ending
y	z	I am pleased with you.	

Letter names 1

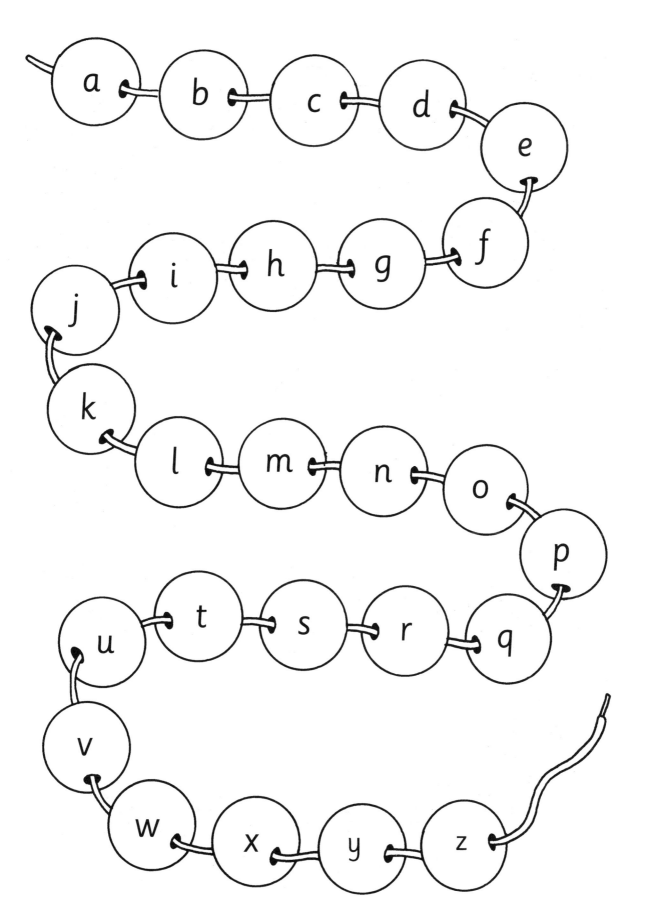

Initial sounds

Fill in the missing letters.

☐op   ☐at   ☐ug

☐in   ☐ap   ☐at

☐ug   ☐en   ☐ig

☐en   ☐in   ☐up

Copymaster 83

Final sounds

Fill in the missing letters.

ba ☐   ja ☐   pa ☐

ca ☐   ta ☐   fa ☐

ba ☐   te ☐   be ☐

bi ☐   ro ☐   su ☐

Medial sounds

Fill in the missing letters.

p □ n   p □ n   t □ b

h □ t   n □ t   j □ g

s □ n   c □ t   t □ p

k □ d   n □ t   p □ g

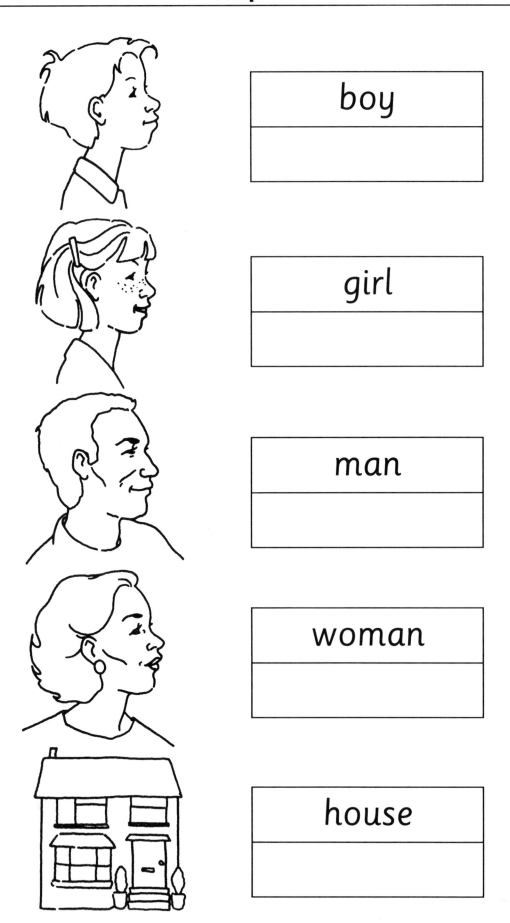

boy

girl

man

woman

house

Matching words

Draw lines to join the matching words.

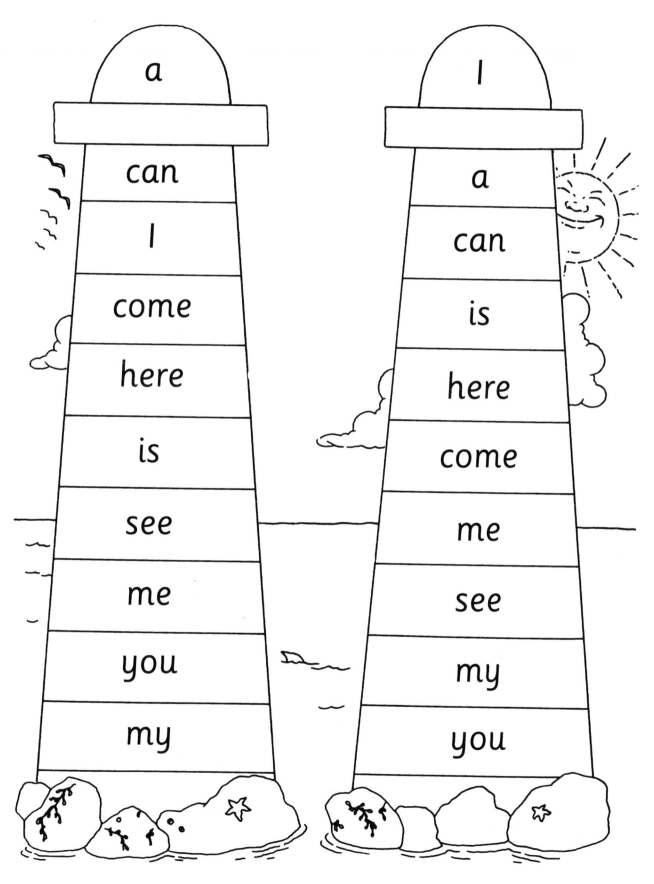

Lighthouse 1	Lighthouse 2
a	I
can	a
I	can
come	is
here	here
is	come
see	me
me	see
you	my
my	you

Draw lines to join the opposites. Use a different colour for each pair.

long   small   cold   sad   closed

large   hot   happy   open   short

Rhyming words

With a line, join the words that rhyme.

 bin

 shed

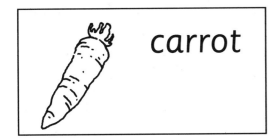 carrot

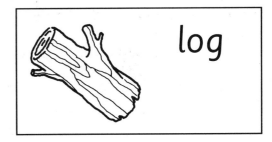 log

 dog

 dish

 fish

 parrot

 rug

 pin

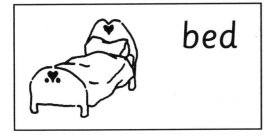 bed

 mug

Tell the story

| 1 | 2 | 3 | 4 | 5 | 6 |

Cut out the pictures. Stick them onto a new sheet of paper in the correct order. Put the numbers beside the pictures in the correct order.

train	swing	hat	sun	dog	apples

The boy is on a

s

I can see a

t

Mum has a new

h

I like the

s

The girl has a little

d

I love to eat

a

I look like this

My name is

I am ☐ years old. I am a | boy | girl |

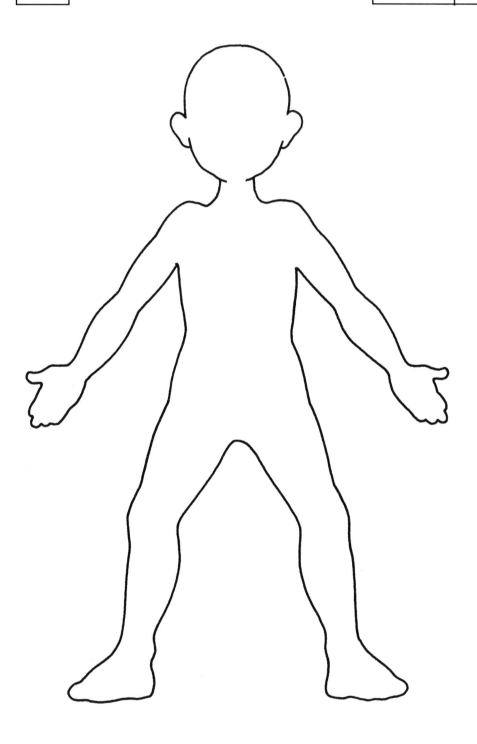

Draw your clothes.   Colour your eyes.
Colour your hair.   Colour your skin.

Things I can do

What can you do?

Tick ✓ if you can do these things.

I can draw. ◯

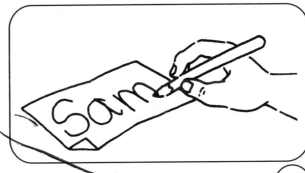

I can write my name. ◯

I can skip. ◯

I can hop. ◯

I can swim. ◯

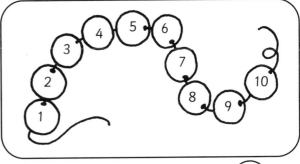

I can count to 10. ◯

I can ride a bike. ◯

I can jump. ◯

The body

Write the words in the correct places and colour the picture.

| head | arm | hand | foot | leg | tummy |

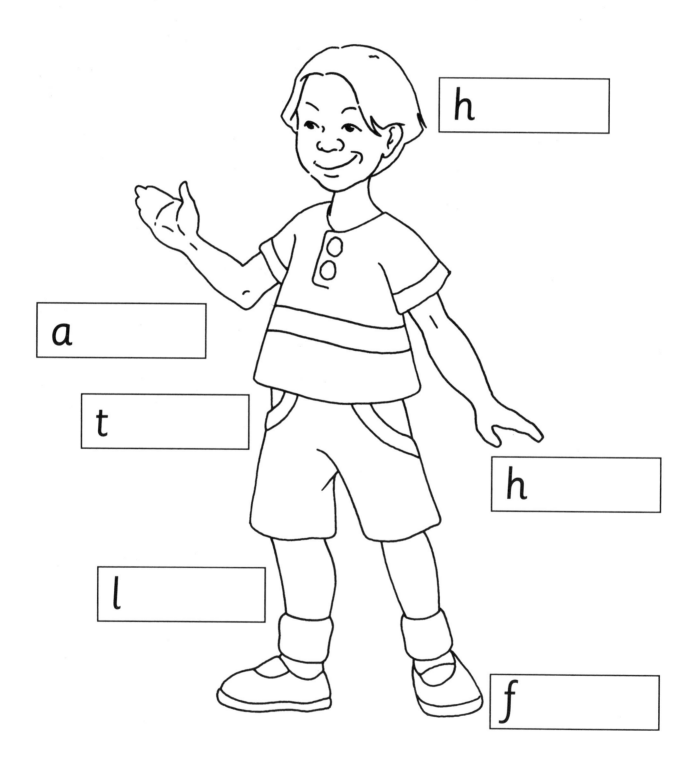

h

a

t

h

l

f

Living and non-living things

Make a set of the living things and colour them in.

Similarities and differences

Use these outlines to draw yourself and a friend.
Talk about the things that are the same.
What can you see that is different?

Colours

Match the colours and numbers to colour the picture.

1 blue	2 red	3 yellow
4 green	5 pink	6 brown

What plants need to live

Add the things this plant needs to live.

Growing things

Use all of these things to grow some cress.

cotton wool

water

Draw what happened.

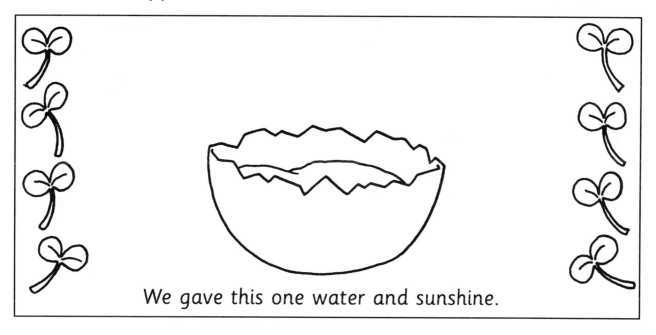

We gave this one water and sunshine.

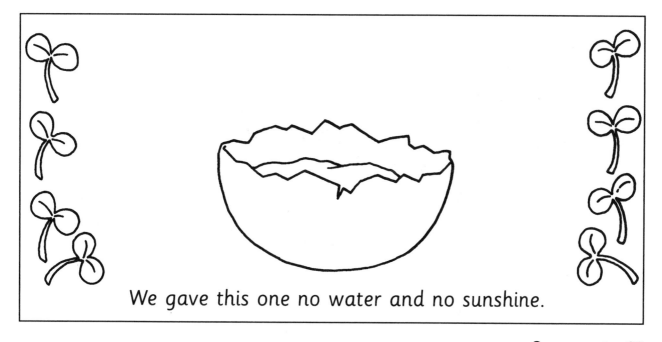

We gave this one no water and no sunshine.

Draw your favourite foods in the circle.
Colour the healthy ones!

I clean my teeth ☐ times a day.

I have a bath or shower ☐ times a week.

I go to bed at ☐ o-clock.

These are my favourite healthy foods.

This is my favourite way of taking exercise.

Weather and clothes

Choose the right clothes for the weather.

Seasons and change

Draw yourself at these different times of the year.
Put in some of the things you might see.

Spring

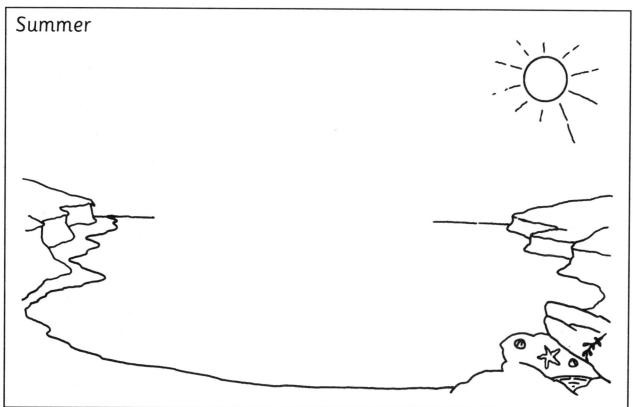

Summer

Seasons and change

Draw yourself at these different times of the year.
Put in some of the things you might see.

Autumn

Winter

Heating changes

Match the pictures to show how heat changes these things.

ice cube   egg   candle   water

fried egg   water   steam   melted wax

Copymaster 105

Cooling changes

Match the pictures to show how cold changes these things.

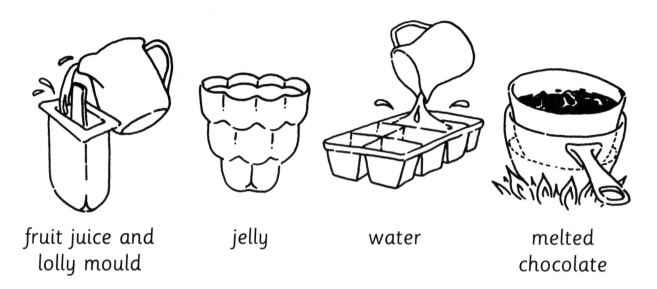

fruit juice and
lolly mould

jelly

water

melted
chocolate

ice cubes

bar of chocolate

jelly

ice lolly

Looking for litter and pollution

Draw a ring around any litter and pollution you can see.

Light and shadow

Tick and colour the things which have the right shadow.

Collecting materials

Find material to go into each one of these boxes.

This is shiny.

This is dull.

This is hard.

This is soft.

This is rough.

This is smooth.

Loud and soft sounds

Colour the pictures of loud sounds $\boxed{\text{red}}$

Colour the pictures of soft sounds $\boxed{\text{blue}}$

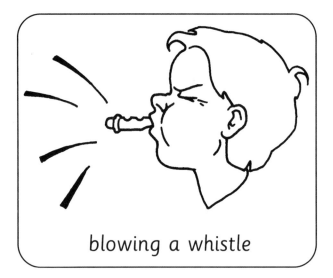

blowing a whistle

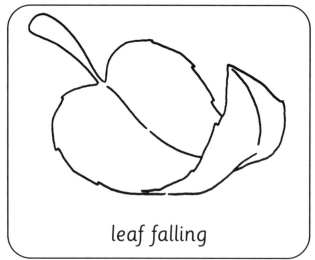

leaf falling

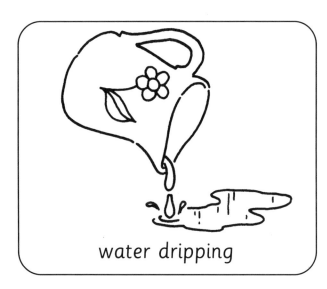

water dripping

alarm clock

scrunching a cloth

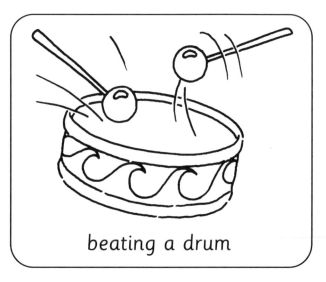

beating a drum

How sounds are made

Tick the box which tells how sounds are made on these instruments.

| s | for strike | p | for pluck | b | for blow | sh | for shake |

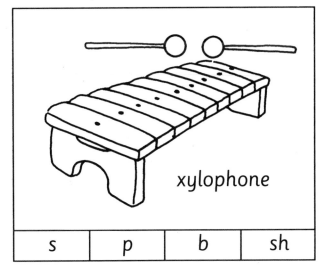

xylophone

| s | p | b | sh |

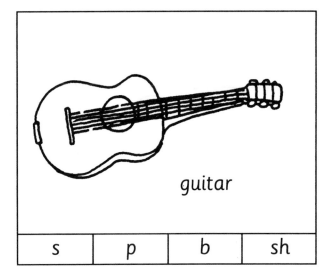

guitar

| s | p | b | sh |

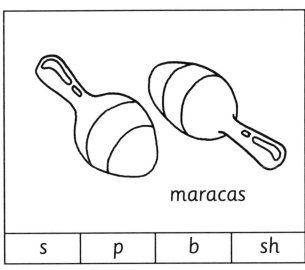

maracas

| s | p | b | sh |

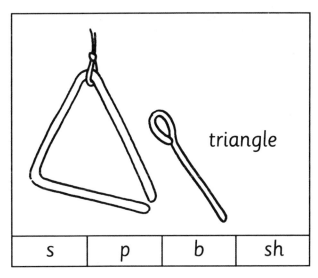

triangle

| s | p | b | sh |

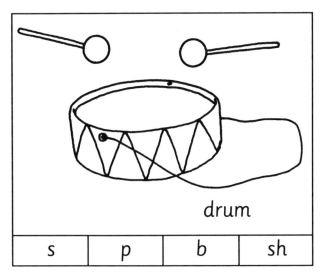

drum

| s | p | b | sh |

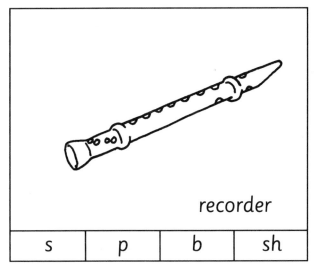

recorder

| s | p | b | sh |

Air power

Sort these things into two sets.
Some are toys which are blown by the wind.
Some are wet clothes to be dried by the wind.

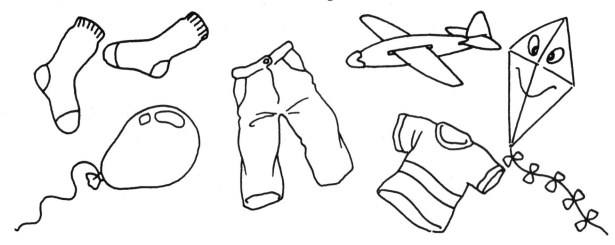

Draw the washing on the line.

Draw the toys on the cloud.

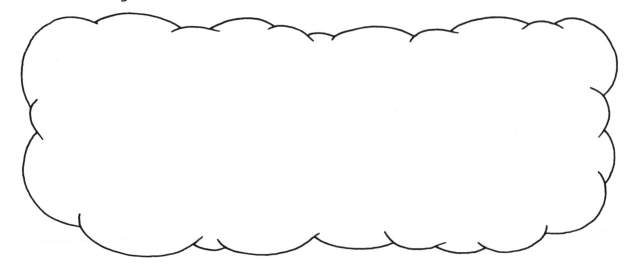

Water power

My water-jet washing-up-liquid bottle.

Tick the box if your jet of water could move these things.

ping-pong ball ☐

toy metal car ☐

flat paper ☐

feather ☐

small pebbles ☐

sand ☐

Floating and sinking

Which of these things float or sink in a tank of water? Cut out the pictures and glue them onto the tank of water to show what happens.

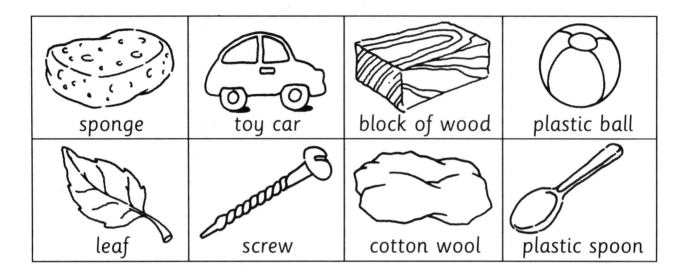

sponge

toy car

block of wood

plastic ball

leaf

screw

cotton wool

plastic spoon

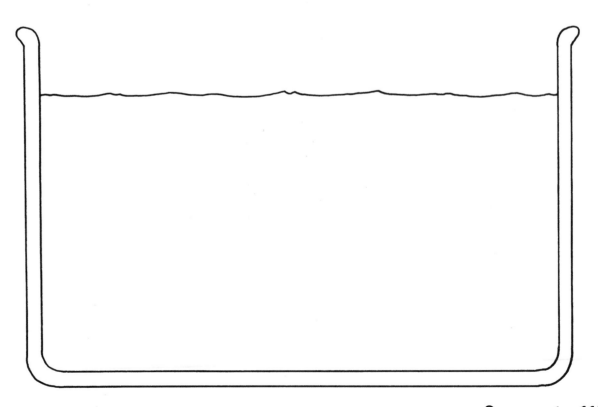

Magnet power

Which of these things are attracted to a magnet?
Join them to the magnet with a line.

plastic comb

ball

glass

paper

key

book

screw

toothbrush

sand

scissors

apple

pin

fork

plastic bottle

knife

metal pen

soft toy

drinks can

paper clip

Pushes and pulls

What do you have to do to move these toys?

toy car

| push | pull | both |

doll's pram

| push | pull | both |

ball

| push | pull | both |

horse on wheels

| push | pull | both |

train

| push | pull | both |

skateboard

| push | pull | both |

Safety in the home – Electricity

Draw a circle around the things which are dangerous.

I know these colours

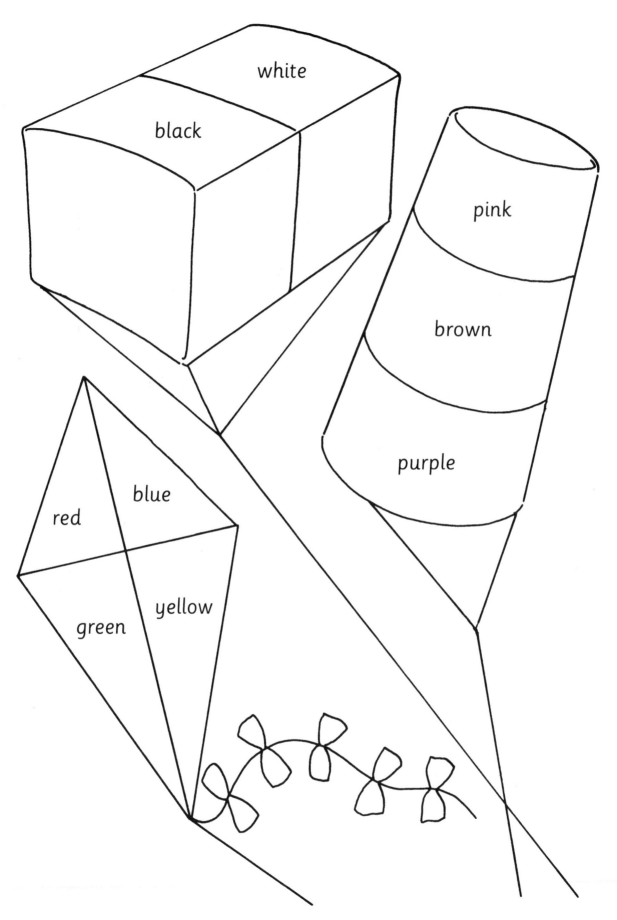

white

black

pink

brown

purple

red

blue

green

yellow

I can write my name

I know these numbers

1 2 3 4 5

I can write them myself.

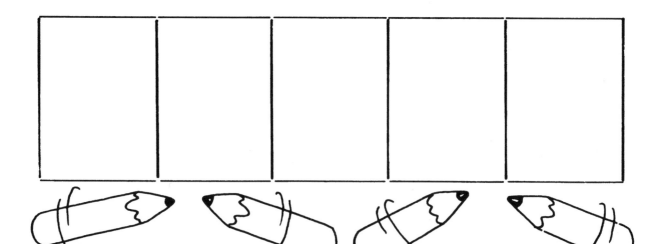

I can draw a special picture

Things I can do

I can dress myself.

I can fasten my shoes.

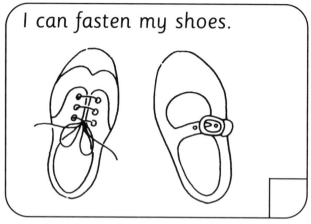

I can put on my own coat.

I can use a knife and fork.

I can fasten my school bag.

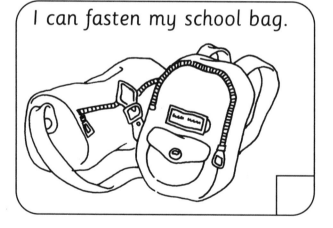

I can wash my hands.

I can go to the toilet myself.

I can use a lunch box.

I can draw myself

Things needed for school

lunch box

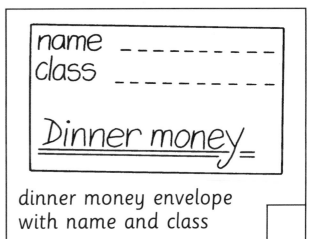

dinner money envelope
with name and class

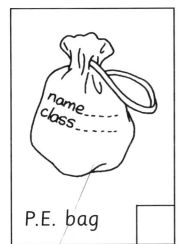

P.E. bag

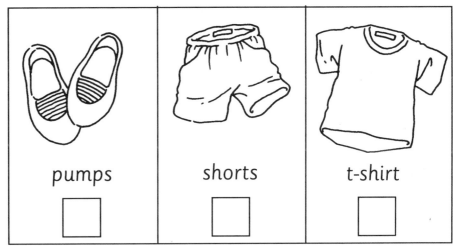

pumps

shorts

t-shirt

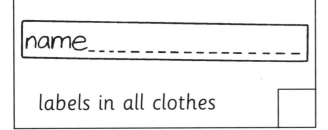

labels in all clothes

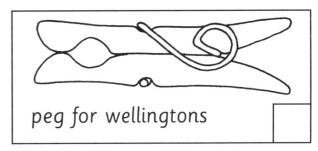

peg for wellingtons

small school
bag

plastic reading
folder

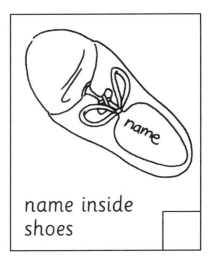

name inside
shoes

Medical/home information sheet

Child's name: .... Date of birth: ....

Address: ....

....

Mother/Guardian: ....

Address, if different: ....

.... Tel. No: ....

Father/Guardian: ....

Address, if different: ....

.... Tel. No: ....

Relative or friend who can be contacted: ....

....

Medical details – Doctor: ....

Address: ....

.... Tel. No: ....

Any medical details you think the school should know about (serious illnesses/allergies).

....

....

....

....

....

....

....

Diary

Name:

This week at school

Date:

Signed:

Diary

Name:

Date:

This week at home

Signed:

Information for parents

School address

School telephone number

Head teacher

The school day
Starts at

break (a.m.)

Lunch

break (p.m.)

Finishes at

Your child's class teacher

_ _ _ _ _ _ _ _ _

Room

When collecting your child for appointments

Number of children in school

_____

Number of children in your child's class

We collect dinner money

My reading record

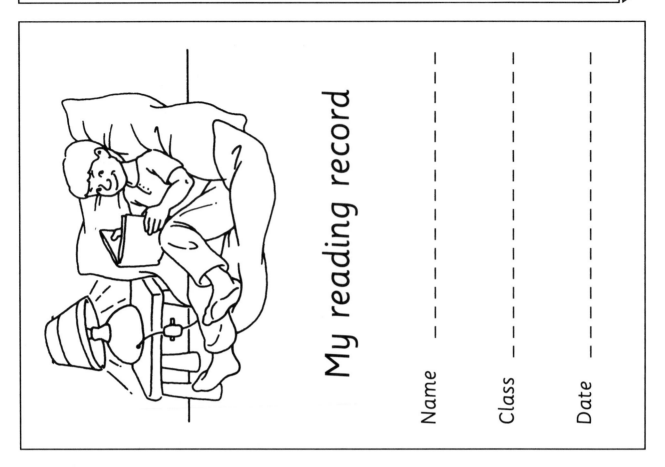

My reading record

Name _ _ _ _ _ _ _ _ _ _ _ _ _ _ _

Class _ _ _ _ _ _ _ _ _ _ _ _ _ _ _

Date _ _ _ _ _ _ _ _ _ _ _ _ _ _ _

Date	Page no.	Title and comments			

Basic mathematic skills

Name .... Class ....

Sort into sets	☐	Partition	☐
Match one-to-one	☐	Record sets	☐
Sequencing (patterns)	☐	Count 1–5	☐

Match numeral and quantity

1   2   3   4   5

Match numeral and quantity

6   7   8   9   10

Write numbers in order 1–10

  1   2   3   4   5   6   7   8   9   10

Recognise number words

  one two three four five six seven eight nine ten

Ordinal numbers

first	second	third	fourth	fifth
1st	2nd	3rd	4th	5th

Plane shapes

3D shapes

Language	higher/ lower	taller/ shorter	big/ small	longer/ shorter

Add one more   ○○○ <u>add one more</u>→ ○○○○

Adding sets

Simple subtraction – Cross one out, how many left?

Basic English skills

Speaking and listening

Listens to a story	Talks to friends	Talks to adults	Joins in group discussions

Handwriting

Tracing	Tracking	Underwriting	Copies from a card	Copies from a board

Letter formation
a b c d e f g h i j k l m n o p q r s t u v w x y z

Reading

Recognises name	Recognises labels	Knows how a book works	Chooses to read a book	Interested in a story

Writing

Attempts to write name	Writes name	Dictates a sentence to a scribe	Uses simple word bank	Emergent writer – attempts own story

Copymaster 132